Pat's Pointers

Pat's Pointers

The Needlepoint Handbook

Pat Trexler

Andrews and McMeel, Inc.
A Universal Press Syndicate Company
Kansas City • New York

Library of Congress Cataloging in Publication Data

Trexler, Pat.
    Pat's pointers.

    Bibliography: p.
    Includes index.
    1. Canvas embroidery.   2. Cross-stitch.   I. Title.
TT778.C3T73   1983   746.44'2   83-2699

ISBN 0-8362-2502-3

Contents

Welcome to the Wonderful World of Needlepoint!

If you already are skilled in needlepoint or counted cross-stitch, it is my hope that I will be able to give you a few tips that might be helpful as well as some patterns and designs that may inspire you.

If you have been wanting to learn, then I hope that my instructions will be clear enough to start you on your merry way to stitchery. If, at first, you feel awkward and your stitches are less than perfect, don't be discouraged. I, too, learned the craft from a "learn-how" book, and I sympathize with your early attempts. Stick with it, though, and I can promise you hours of sheer delight as you take needle, canvas, and yarn and create items of lasting beauty.

No book of this sort can be written without the help of many people, and I would be remiss in not acknowledging some of those who made it possible.

First, of course, I give thanks to my Heavenly Father who gifted me with the talent to use my hands and the opportunities to share my thoughts and ideas with you.

To my husband, Jack—ever patient when meals were late and the house was cluttered with yarn—for his constant love and encouragement in all I do and for the long hours spent behind the camera and in the darkroom creating most of the photographs appearing in this book.

To my children, Connie, Jim, Jack, Jr., and Tom and my grandchildren, Brent, Paul, Tammy, Stacy, Jason, and Kevin for being a source of joy.

To Margaret Brainard, Cam Burdick, Clara Carran, Vivian Conway, Chris Harrelson, Kay Johnson, Georgia Kasun, Mary Jo Trout, Terry Williams, and Marie Whitaker—the staff in our office who process all the mail, send you leaflets and kits, handle the myriad of details from day to day, and encourage me in so many ways.

To the newspapers throughout the country that carry my column as a weekly feature.

To John McMeel, Tom Thornton, Lee Salem, Lisa Michels, Donna Martin, and all of the rest of the great staff at Universal Press Syndicate who edit, distribute, and promote my column.

To Betty Hill and Millie Adams, who knit and crochet some of the items you see in my column, and to Mike Borders and Elmo Carroll who have contributed needlepoint items.

To Mildred Elwell, Jeanette Schmell, Pauline Asmus, Mary Becker, Toni Urbaitis, Ginny Thompson, Barbara Seres, Susan Strange, Elaine McArn, Peggy McConnel, Virginia Ross, Harriet Hirsch, and various others who have shared their designs over the years.

To my fellow members of the American Needlepoint Guild, with special thanks to Marty Pugh, Faye Sheridan, Maxine Graham, Chottie Alderson, Bill and Mabel Doser, Pat White, Connie Binns, Evelyn Sayer, Mary Jane Briscoe, Myrl Good.

To needlecraft authors Mary Gostelow, Barbara Walker, Liz Blackwell, Jean Riley, Nancy Hall, Hope Hanley, Gertrude Taylor, Jo Bucher, Jo Christensen—and the many others listed in the bibliography—all of whom have been a source of inspiration to me.

To all of the above and to stitchery lovers everywhere, this book is dedicated.

Getting Down to Basics

I never met the author of this little epistle—I simply found it in a little pamphlet given out at the American Pro-Cathedral in Paris several years ago while viewing the cathedral's needlepoint kneelers.

"It's an old-fashioned cure for restlessness, my dear, in case you ever need it. Remember that it has been successful for hundreds of people. I'm no fool, am I? Well, I haven't traveled without my tapestry since my girlhood and you should see the splendid suites of furniture covered by my handiwork, testimonials to worries of all sorts.

"Whenever I have felt nervous, vaguely dissatisfied, irresolute or frankly wretched, I have sat by myself and stitched. Each embroidery contains hundreds of stitches which are the cross-stones of sorrow, the death beds of boredom.

"In many a gaily flowered seat, my unhappiness lies buried. People spend time and money being exorcised; psychoanalysed, they call it, seeking relief for body and soul.

"I think that a good long mechanical task that requires a minimum of attention and the soothing action of the hand as it dips over and under the canvas, is the very best means of pinning down our weaknesses and chloroforming them.

"Stitch the horrors down, my dear, and they shan't return to plague you; they are killed by a stab of the needle.

"Of course, during some peaceful interludes, I have laid my work aside for a time, but when I need it—there it is—as convenient as a box of aspirin for a cold." —Anne Green, Paris, France.

I'm sure that all needlecrafters, whether they needlepoint, knit, crochet, or embroider, will find a world of truth in her words. Most of us, however, don't put aside our needlework in happy times—we just stitch away, serene and blissful!

Because she refers to "a good long mechanical task that requires a minimum of attention," I have to believe that most of her needlepoint was background filling around pre-worked centers.

While there is much to be said for that type of work—particularly its soothing effects—there is much more excitement in today's needlepoint, and most of us who become truly addicted to needlepoint find the greatest delight in starting with blank canvas and working in a variety of stitches.

Working in this fashion makes needlepoint more affordable, too. When you are working background around an already worked center design, you are paying for the many hours it took for someone to stitch the design. The same is true, although often to a lesser degree, of stitching a painted canvas.

From time to time, I have heard people say: "I would never have the patience to do that!" While it is true that you are not likely to sit down and complete most needlepoint projects in an evening or two, most are so fascinating that it is not a matter of patience at all. In fact, most of us who do work of this type are impatient people who can't sit with idle hands.

An extremely talented needlepoint designer and instructor, Diane Kleinman of Canoga Park, California, in reply to a request for a short biography, once wrote: "I am a native Californian who loves and enjoys every day of life. I love to laugh, to enjoy, to try new things—especially anything dealing with arts, crafts, or new concepts in design. I am young at heart, have a zest for life, and am particularly happy with my husband and three beautiful daughters.

"Teaching stitchery to handicapped children has been a special treat for me, but I also teach those without handicaps—adults and children. But I particularly love the spontaneity in children when they design and create.

"A philosophy that I like to share with the people I teach is that everyone can design and create. People just need to become aware of all the beauty around them. Design is everywhere! Nature has the most exquisite color combinations anyone could ask for!

"Needlecraft is beautiful to see, a pleasure to enjoy, and fun to do. It is here to stay! There's always a new stitch, a new concept, and something exciting to work on tomorrow!"

Before we get down to basics, I would like to share one last quote with you from another leading teacher-designer, Chottie Alderson of Running Springs, California.

Like most of us heavily involved in stitchery, Chottie has a house full of yarn, canvas, and half-finished projects—and a lot of half-finished housework as well. In self-defense, she once stitched up this motto, "A clean house is the sign of misspent life!"

NEEDLES AND YARN

Needles used for needlepoint are called tapestry needles and have large eyes and blunt points. The correct needle size is determined by the canvas and yarn you are using. Below is a chart listing a suggested needle size for various sizes of canvas. Often, though, you will have a supply of needles and will have no idea of the size of each. A good rule of thumb is to select the smallest size needle that can easily be threaded with the yarn you are using. A needle that is too large for the canvas can cause you to force the needle through the canvas, resulting in jerky motions that destroy an even tension. **Tapestry Needles**

MESH COUNT	NEEDLE SIZE
3	14
5	14
6	16
7	18
10	20
12	20
14	22
16	24

Often the biggest obstacle for the beginner is the seemingly simple act of threading the needle. The "lick-and-twist" method used with sewing thread simply won't work. **Threading the Needle**

There are needle threaders available at most craft counters designed for the large eyes of tapestry needles. Or you can simply cut a small rectangle of paper, fold it in half lengthwise, and place the end of the yarn in the fold. Then just push the folded end through the eye and the yarn will pop through at the same time.

I strongly suggest, though, that you try to learn the following method so you can always quickly thread your needle wherever you are without having to keep up with a threader or even a scrap of paper.

Fold the end of the yarn over the fat part of the needle and

5

pinch the resulting fold between the thumb and forefinger. Draw the needle out and push the eye of the needle *down* onto the folded yarn. If you do this correctly the yarn will just pop right into the eye.

Securing Yarn Ends

Regular readers of my column know that I am not a perfectionist who believes there is only one right way to achieve good results in any form of needlework. I do, however, have one unbreakable rule for any type of embroidery, which includes needlepoint. You should never have any little short, loose ends dangling on the wrong side of your work. This is not just because you will have a messy looking wrong side, but these loose ends are sure to get caught up in future stitches, causing lumps and knots that will affect the right side of your work.

To avoid this, you should always have a pair of scissors handy and snip every loose end close to your work *after* you have secured the yarn. To secure your yarn, pull the threaded needle through a few unworked stitches on the wrong side each time you start or finish with a strand.

The only time you might find this a problem is when you prepare to take your first stitch on a blank piece of canvas. There are no stitches there, so what do you do! A little trick I learned from Marion Scoular of Clemson, South Carolina, many years ago has served me well and will be invaluable to you. It's the "waste-knot" technique. Although knots in your yarn are a big "no-no" in needlepoint, I will tell you to start your first strand with a knot. Before you gasp, let me assure you that we will quickly get rid of that knot!

When you have made a knot in the end of your yarn, take the needle down through the canvas from the right side of your work to the wrong side of your work, a few holes away from the point where you will take your first stitch—in the direction in which you will be stitching.

For example, if your first stitch will be in the upper right corner and you will be stitching from right to left, count over about 10 holes to the left of the corner and position the knot there. Now, as you stitch from right to left, you will be covering the part of the strand that extends from the knot to the first stitch, thus securing it as you stitch. When you come near the knot, snip it off, and stitch merrily away!

The only time you are likely to use more than one knot on a single piece of canvas is when you are leaving areas of the background unworked, as you would do with colored canvas, for example. In this event, you do not want strands of yarn extending from one design area to another under unworked canvas, so you would start with a waste knot each time you begin a new section.

Yarn Lengths

Probably because they dislike frequent threading of the needle, one of the most common mistakes made by beginners—and even some old-timers—is the use of too long a strand of yarn in the needle. How long is too long? Well, to begin with, if you are having to stretch your arm every time you take a stitch, the yarn is far too long. But even if you have a comfortable working length, it could still be too long for your particular project.

There are very good reasons for using fairly short lengths of yarn. Each time you pull the yarn through the canvas, tiny yarn fibers cling to the canvas, thus wearing the yarn thin. This is not usually obvious to the human eye, but it is surely occurring. Therefore, the stitches you take with the beginning of a new strand will be "fatter" than those taken near the end of the strand and your work will have a very uneven texture.

The mesh count of your canvas and the type of stitch you are using are both factors in determining the correct length. With a fine canvas, you will be taking more stitches per inch than will be the case with a large-mesh canvas. Therefore, you would use a shorter length on 14-mesh than you would on 7-mesh. If you are working with pattern stitches that pass over several threads of canvas with each stitch, you can work with a longer strand than you would use with tent stitches.

Probably about the shortest you would ever use would be 16 to 18 inches and the longest, even with Bargello on large mesh canvas, would be approximately 32 inches.

Nap and Grain

Did you know that yarn has a nap or grain? This is true and it can have an effect on the appearance of your stitches. If you are using tapestry yarn, packaged in pull-out skeins, it's a simple matter to always have the nap in the right direction. Just remember to thread your needle with the end of the yarn as it pulls from the center.

With other types of yarn, you'll need to learn to recognize the direction of the nap by feel. Many people can do this by running the yarn between their thumb and forefinger. It will feel smooth in one direction and rough in another.

Hold the yarn so that it is smooth from top to bottom and thread the top end into your needle.

I have heard teachers say, "Anyone can feel the nap." However, at one time, I temporarily experienced a slight numbness in my fingers and lost the sensitivity that allowed me to do this, so I know that some of you will be unable to determine the nap in that way.

A friend who was also a needlepoint instructor had the same problem which she solved by running the strand of yarn under her nose—it tickles more when going against the grain or nap! Much of my stitchery is done in public places and I couldn't quite cope with the puzzled stares when doing this. I discovered a more acceptable method of testing by rubbing the strands across my cheek.

Woven canvas also has a grain. If you will look closely at the canvas, you will see that one mesh will have a vertical thread on top and the next will have a horizontal thread on top.

When you are doing the basketweave stitch, your work will be more even if you work with the grain. In this stitch, your work progresses up from right to left and down from left to right.

Your upward row should be worked over the meshes with the horizontal thread on top and your downward rows should be worked over the meshes with the vertical thread on top.

As You Sew, So Shall You Rip

If you are a beginner, you may not know that you need to "beware of the fuzzies!"

Almost any stitcher must occasionally rip out a few stitches, but what many do not realize is that whenever you do so, fibers from the yarn will cling to the canvas. This wouldn't matter so much except that these fibers then have a tendency to work their way into the new stitches you take in the same area and that does create a problem when you add a new color in that area or an adjacent one.

These often tenacious fibers have a way of showing up on the right side of your work and are almost impossible to pick out. Fortunately, however, there is an easy solution. Just wrap some masking tape around your fingers—sticky side out—and pat over the area where the stitches were ripped. Those pesky fibers will then adhere to the tape and will cause you no further trouble.

The fact that fibers do stick to the canvas illustrates why you should work with relatively short lengths of yarn at all times.

The easiest way to rip out is one stitch at a time, working back from the last stitch taken. Just slip the needle off of the yarn and use the needle tip to pull out each stitch.

Sometimes, however, you will have a large area to rip or you might need to rip an area surrounded by stitches that will be left in. In either of these cases, you will need to cut the stitches. This should be done with great care so that you do not cut the canvas. Use a very small pair of sharp pointed embroidery scissors. I find it easier to cut the stitches from the right side. Even after you have cut the stitches, you will find some that do not pull out easily. This usually occurs at the places where you have secured the yarn under some stitches or where you have split the stitches with your needle. I have no quick cure for this. It is simply a tedious, uninteresting task.

Before you rip, however, be sure that it is absolutely necessary. Sometimes a mistake can turn into an original design!

WORKING FROM CHARTS

Working needlepoint designs from graph charts can be rewarding in more ways than one. In these days of ever-rising prices, perhaps the most important reason for learning how to do this is that it is by far the most economical way to have lovely needlepoint pieces.

If you buy needlepoint canvas with the design worked, with only the background to be done by you, you are paying for someone's time in working the design. And, while such pieces are usually imported from countries with low wage scales, this still adds a considerable amount to the cost.

Canvases with hand-painted designs are often the most expensive, but even those with the design stamped or printed on them will cost you more than those that you work from graph charts.

To many avid stitchers, however, the most important plus is that wonderful feeling of accomplishment and satisfaction that you have when you start with just a blank piece of canvas and a "palette" of luscious yarn colors and create something of lasting beauty with your needle.

As an example of how another needlepointer feels, let me share with you a letter I received from one reader:

Dear Pat: Would you devote a column to the use of charts for needlepoint and cross-stitch? For years I deprived myself of much pleasure because I was sure that I couldn't follow such charts. I finally took the plunge a few months ago when I saw some charted butterflies that were irresistible. Now, I can't find enough hours in the day to work all of the charts I have collected. I'm sure there are many others who are intimidated by the very idea of charted needlework and who would be delighted to learn how easy this type of work really is.—Sue B., Colorado Springs, Colorado.

If you have never worked from a chart, why not read this section and give it a try. Like Sue, you will probably end up hooked on chartwork!

There are two basic types of charts—design charts and stitch charts—which will be discussed separately.

Design Charts A design chart is almost a picture of the finished design, usually pictorial in nature. For an example of this type of chart, turn to p. 113 and look at the Cardinal Wastebasket Cover Design.

Each symbol on the chart represents one stitch to be taken. If more than one symbol is used, each symbol will denote a different color. For example, everywhere the symbol • appears, one stitch is to be taken with bright red yarn.

Each square of the graph chart paper represents one hole of the canvas and each line on the paper represents a thread of canvas. (Remember that the ribs of plastic canvas are also referred to as "threads.") Sometimes the symbols appear in the squares (as in the cardinal design) and sometimes they are shown crossing the lines.

When the symbols are shown in squares, this corresponds to the hole in the canvas where you bring the needle up to start the stitch. When the symbols cross the line, this corresponds to the mesh that is crossed by the stitch. Either method is easy to follow when you become accustomed to it.

Let's say you have your canvas, yarn, needle, and chart . . . ready to begin, but where do you start. In most instances, it is best to start in the center to be sure that the design will be positioned properly. So we need to find the center of the chart and the canvas.

If your chart is not marked to show you the center, here's how you go about finding it on your own. Find the row where the very top stitch symbol appears and mark that row with a pencil. Now do the same at the bottom of the chart. Fold the chart so that the top and bottom pencil lines meet. The crease of the fold will be your horizontal center. Next mark the rows where the far right and far left stitch symbols appear and fold so that these pencil lines meet. The crease will be your vertical center. Where the two fold lines meet will be your chart center. Circle the stitch symbol at the center.

Next, let's find the center of your canvas. You don't want crease lines in traditional canvas and plastic canvas *won't* crease, so use sewing thread to baste the center lines. Gently fold the canvas lengthwise and run the basting line along the fold; then fold it in the other direction and again run a basting line. The point where the basting threads cross is the center of your fabric.

Take your first stitch in the canvas center with the stitch shown on the chart center, using the waste-knot technique described on p. 6-7. From this point you can work up, down, right, or left. I usually prefer to work from the center down and then, turning canvas and chart upside down, work from center to top.

Some people—and I am one of these—prefer to work all areas of one color and then do the same with all remaining colors. Others thread needles with each color to be used and change back and forth, working straight across, changing colors each time a symbol changes.

You will also want to know the finished size of your design. If this information is not provided, you can easily figure this out yourself. This will vary according to the mesh size of your canvas.

After you have marked the center stitch, count across the number of squares from the center at the widest point of the design area and do the same at the deepest point of the design area. Double each of these numbers.

Example: If there are 48 squares from the center across to one edge, the design area is 96 squares wide. If there are 36 squares from the center to the top or bottom, the design area will be 72 squares deep. Now, if your canvas is a 12-mesh size, your finished design will cover an area 8 inches (96 divided by 12) in width and 6 inches (72 divided by 12) in depth. However, if your canvas was a 6-mesh size, the finished design area would be 16 inches by 12 inches as you would be dividing the same figures by six rather than 12.

The same principle will apply regardless of your mesh size. Just remember that this will give you the size of the design area only, without taking into consideration the amount of background area you will want.

It is always a good idea to start with a larger canvas than you think you will need, in case you are a little off center when you start or you decide to enlarge on some area of the design as you work.

With traditional canvas, remember to allow for the necessary unworked margins of an inch or two around *all* edges for hems or blocking. No extra margins are needed for plastic canvas, but I suggest that you not cut the canvas to size until your design area is complete in case you need extra canvas on any side.

As mentioned earlier, one of the principal reasons for working on blank canvas is the economy of it, but of equal importance is the choice of color and size.

Generally speaking, with a painted or stamped canvas, you should stick with the colors selected by the designer. If you try to stitch a lighter color over a dark area, the results are seldom good. And, of course, you cannot change the finished size.

Stitch Charts These are basically diagrams that show you the direction, or slant, of the stitches and the number of threads and holes over which each stitch passes.

The solid chart lines represent the threads (or ribs) of the canvas and the blank squares represent the holes of the canvas. There are two general numbering systems used. (1) The needle is brought up in odd numbered holes and taken down in even numbered holes. Example: Bring the needle up at #1, take it down at #2; up at #3, down at #4; up at #5 and down at #6 and so on. (2) Arrows are used and numbers may appear only where the needle comes up from the wrong to the right side of the work with arrow points showing you where the needle goes down into the canvas.

The tent stitch, usually thought of as the basic needlepoint stitch, is usually not numbered on pictorial design charts, but is often illustrated with numbers in teaching diagrams. This simple stitch, diagonally crossing one mesh of the canvas, can be worked in various ways. The most common are the half-cross, continental, and basketweave. While all three appear much the same on the front (or right side) of the canvas, each looks quite different on the back. Refer to the stitch charts for half-cross and continental on p. 30. These charts look identical except for the position of the numbers.

While the stitches themselves lay in the same direction, the numbers tell you that your working direction is different for each. In the half-cross you are working from right to left, while in the continental you are working from left to right. If you try out each stitch following the charts, you will be able to see the difference for yourself.

The same is true of the basketweave stitch. Many beginners find this difficult to learn, but if you follow the numbers carefully, you should be able to master it readily.

Now, look at the basketweave stitch chart. As you can see, this is worked diagonally rather than horizontally or vertically, but the numbering sequence is equally important.

Decorative—or pattern—stitches can be used as accents or as overall design elements. Each decorative stitch will consist of two or more stitches worked in varying ways. The charts for such stitches are worked by following the numbered sequences.

Canvas

For centuries, needlepoint canvas was made of natural fibers, primarily cotton. In recent years, new technologies have given us needlepoint canvas in polyesters and plastic. In discussing the various types, I will refer to the natural fiber canvases as "traditional." Although actually not traditional, the polyesters fall into this same category, as they require fairly much the same treatment as the natural fiber canvas. The various new forms of plastic canvas will be considered nontraditional.

TRADITIONAL CANVAS

In traditional canvas, there are two general categories—penelope and mono. The penelope has closely woven double threads both vertically and horizontally, while mono has single threads in each direction.

Categories

In past years most canvas was of the penelope type, but it is much less common today. Its primary use is in combining gros point and petit point stitches on one piece. These are both tent stitches (see stitch charts on p. 30) with the larger gros point stitches worked over the double threads and the petit point stitches worked by splitting the threads and working one stitch over each.

In the mono category, you will find woven and interlocked canvases. Because there is much difference of opinion among experts as to which of these is better, I suggest that, if you are a serious needlepointer, you should experiment with both and select the one that better meets your needs or that gives you the better results.

The interlock is my choice, particularly for Bargello, but there are many who would disagree with me. However, woven canvas is more durable and therefore it would be the better choice for an item that will get a great deal of wear over a number of years.

Preparing the Canvas

When you are buying blank canvas, you should always allow for a 1- to 2-inch unworked margin around all sides of a piece. For example, if you want a finished pillow of 14 inches by 14 inches, you should start with a piece at least 16 inches by 16 inches and an 18-inch by 18-inch piece would be even better. You will need some of this for turning under or seaming, but, more importantly, you will need a large margin when you are blocking.

Before you take the first stitch, you should prepare the edges to prevent raveling and to keep from having rough raw edges that can scratch your fingers or catch on your clothing. You can cover these edges with masking tape or turn under and stitch in a hem. With some canvas, you can even turn under and press in a hem with your iron.

Marking the Canvas

There are times that you will need to mark the canvas—usually for design placement. Whenever possible, I recommend that you mark with basting threads. These can be pulled out later without leaving a trace. If you must use a marker, be *absolutely* certain that the marker is waterproof. If you do not take this precaution, disaster can set in when you block, wash, or clean the piece and the markings bleed onto your finished needlepoint. I don't even recommend the use of a pencil as the graphite from the lead can soil your yarn as it is pulled through the canvas where you have marked.

Distortion

With many needlepoint stitches, traditional canvas will distort or go on the bias. This is the primary reason for blocking—to straighten the canvas back to its original shape. In the case of severe distortion, even extensive blocking will not restore it to perfect shape. There are ways to lessen the distortion, but, with some stitches, it is almost impossible to eliminate it.

One of the best ways to avoid distortion is by working your needlepoint on a frame using the "stab" technique with an easy tension. Many needlepointers won't even consider the use of a frame, however, feeling that it slows them down and makes their needlepoint less "portable." If you hate tedious blocking as I do, however, you will prefer working on a frame.

Selection of Stitches

Any needlepoint stitch can be used on traditional canvas. Some are better suited for the woven type while others work best on the interlock. The various stitches will be described and diagrammed later in the book. Generally speaking, the interlock is preferable for the long straight stitches used in Bargello and Gobelin or Norweave stitchery, while woven canvas must be used for "pulled" work when you are trying to achieve a lacy effect. Penelope is usually not the best choice for pattern stitches, but if the mesh size you wish to use is not available in mono, penelope will have to be used.

Many expert needlepointers use a wide variety of yarn and threads, varying them to get the desired textures. Generally speaking, however, the most commonly used are the tapestry wools and Persian yarns.

Yarn Choices

Tapestry wool is tightly twisted while Persian yarn has three loosely twisted plies. The big advantage to Persian or Persian-type yarn is that you can easily use any number of plies—or strands—in any given situation.

As mentioned earlier, needlepoint canvas comes in many sizes identified by the number of meshes to the inch. A mesh is the intersection or crossing of one vertical and one horizontal thread over which a single stitch is taken.

Depending on the tension of your stitches, tapestry yarn may work beautifully with tent stitches on 12-mesh or 14-mesh canvas, but might be too thick for 16-mesh or too thin for 10-mesh. If you are using Persian yarn, you can use one or two plies for finer canvas and four or more for coarser canvas.

The type of stitch you use can also determine the number of strands used. Straight Bargello or Gobelin stitches usually require more strands for good coverage than do the small, slanting tent stitches. Some raised stitches, such as Smyrna, Rhodes, or double leviathan, take fewer strands for good coverage.

It is a good idea to take a few practice stitches in the margin of your canvas to see that the coverage is good and that the effect is what you desire.

The yarn should be thin enough so that the stitches lie smoothly side by side and the needle passes easily through the holes in the canvas. It should be thick enough, however, to cover the canvas completely.

There are a couple of pointers I should give you about working with Persian yarns. Even if you will be using all three strands, you should first separate them and then place them together again. This is known as "stripping" the yarn. If you do not strip it, the yarn will twist too much, causing uneven stitches. It is extremely important to use this stripping technique when working with straight stitches.

Regardless of the type of yarn you use, you should be careful not to let it twist excessively as you stitch. Anytime it seems to have twisted on itself too much, simply drop the needle and let the needle and yarn dangle below your work and the twists will come out. Or just get in the habit of giving the needle a little counterclockwise twirl after every three or four stitches.

While it helps with any stitch to keep the yarn flat, it is even more important when working long straight stitches. When doing any type of Bargello, I hold the strands down with my left thumb at the base of the last stitch taken. This may sound like a bother, but it is worth it when you see the difference it makes in the beauty of the finished piece.

While seemingly quite expensive, Persian yarns can be more economical in pieces where small quantities of a number of colors are used as these yarns can often be purchased by the strand, avoiding the need to buy complete skeins.

You may wonder if there are any advantages to tapestry wool. I think there are. If the tapestry wool covers the canvas satisfactorily, I find that smoother stitches result, particularly for the beginner. Also the stripping process is eliminated, saving you a little time.

My best advice would be not to limit yourself to any one type of yarn, but to experiment and use whatever gives you the best results for any given project. Odds and ends of leftover yarns can often create exciting effects.

Blocking and Finishing

When you have completed any needlepoint piece, you should work a couple of extra rows of tent stitches around all the outer edges whether you are going to have it professionally blocked and finished or do it yourself, unless it is to be put together with a binding stitch. With a binding stitch finish, this is not done.

Then, check it carefully and be sure that all of the stitching is complete. By holding it up to a light or a window, you can tell if you might have skipped some stitches here and there. If you have, go back and fill them in now.

If you are going to have the piece finished by professional finishers, it's time to turn it over to them. Most professional finishers prefer to do their own blocking. If you have marked the canvas in any way or if it was a painted canvas, be sure to give this information to the finisher. (See comments on marking the canvas on p. 14.)

BLOCKING If your canvas piece has distorted—or gone on the bias—don't panic! That is not at all unusual with traditional canvas, and, unless it is an unusually severe case, you can take care of it with blocking. In extreme cases you might need to have it professionally blocked.

In choosing a professional blocker, don't assume that any dry cleaner can do this for you. Many otherwise expert dry cleaning establishments do not have the expertise for handling fine needlepoint. You might ask some of your needlepointing friends who have had professional blocking done for recommendations. The safest option—and the most economical—is to do your own blocking.

Admittedly, this can be a tedious task but it is not too difficult for the average person. The main purpose of blocking is to restore the piece to its original shape.

For the blocking process, you will need a firm surface, preferably one that is soft enough to push pins into. If your surface won't take pins, you will have to be sure to obtain rust-proof tacks or nails. A building supply store is a good source of insulation board or "soft board" and most will sell you small pieces. The board should then be marked with 1-inch squares in a waterproof ink. Or, for a one-time blocking, mark the outline of the desired shape of the finished object, taking great care to see that all lines are straight and all corners squared. Or, better yet, cover the board with woven gingham and you can use the gingham squares in lining up your piece.

In addition to the board, you will need rust-proof pins. It is very important that any pins, nails, or tacks used are rust-proof as you will be dampening the needlepoint piece and certainly do not want any rust stains. Most needlepoint shops have "T-pins" that are designed for this, or you can use wig pins.

There is some disagreement among experts as to when and how to dampen the piece. Some will tell you to dampen first and then start pinning; others recommend pinning first and then dampening. Some insist that steam works best; some adhere to the idea of lightly moistening with a fine spray of cool water; some roll a piece in a damp towel for a few hours while others recommend a complete soaking.

Steam or soaking, however, can be overdone by the inexperienced blocker, so I would recommend one of the other two methods.

If the piece is only slightly distorted, you can usually pin it to shape and then dampen it. Otherwise, I find it more practical to dampen first and then pin in place. In the following directions, I will assume that you will dampen first.

To me, spraying is the easiest method. Take a clean glass or plastic bottle with a spray attachment and fill it with cool tap water. Now, spray the piece lightly until it is evenly moist all over.

If you choose to roll it in a towel, I suggest that you dampen the towel evenly by tossing it in the washing machine and running it through a quick rinse and spin cycle so that the moisture is evenly distributed. Roll the piece in the towel and leave it for an hour or so.

After your piece is dampened you will pin it to shape on your blocking surface. Again, there is a difference of opinion in pinning the needlepoint down. Some say to do it face up, others say "Never face up, always face down!" So rest easy and know whichever you decide, you will have an expert on your side. Personally, I prefer the "face-up" school of thought.

Start at the upper left corner with the corner of the needle-point lined up with a corner of the gingham or the marked inch lines, placing the pins in the *unworked* margin of canvas—never into the stitched area. Now, working across the top edge, place the pins in the margin at ½-inch intervals, pulling at the edge to keep it lined up with the straight edges of the blocking surface. Place about three pins very close to the upper right corner. Now, go back to the upper left corner and place extra pins in this corner also. Next, work down to the lower left corner, again pulling and tugging to get the edges straight and even.

After securing this corner with the three pins, work on the right edge of the canvas. Depending upon the amount of bias distortion you have, you may have to spend a lot of time or effort straightening this edge, but stick with it until it is perfectly straight. Place three pins at this corner. Finally, place the pins at ½-inch intervals along the lower edge.

When you are sure that the piece is exactly square, leave it to dry for a couple of days away from any direct sunlight. Don't try to hurry the drying process. When you are certain that the piece is completely dry, it is time to take the pins out and think about assembling the needlepoint into a finished piece.

FINISHING Complete books have been written on the subject of finishing techniques, so I obviously cannot include them all in this chapter. The finishing of simple projects, however, can be done by most needlepointers and here are some helpful hints for you.

One of the most useful stitches for finishing is the binding stitch, which should be practiced on a scrap of canvas before attempting to finish any given project. One of the clearest sets of illustrations and directions that I have ever found for this stitch is in the book, *Bargello Borders* by Nancy Hall and Jean Riley. With their permission, I am reproducing both here.

The binding stitch is a flat woven braid that is worked over the

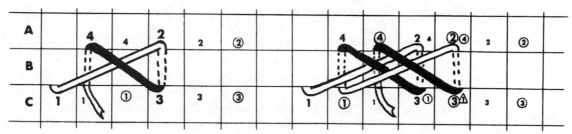

Binding Stitch #1

folded edge of the canvas. It is worked in a straight line, but can be carried around a square corner. I would not recommend it for curved lines or uneven edges.

The Hall-Riley approach to teaching this stitch is to suggest that you first practice it as a decorative surface stitch rather than as an edging until you are comfortable with the stitch progression. In this type of practice, Row B is never used. You will be working on Rows A and C only.

Begin by bringing your needle up at 1.

Carry yarn forward to 2. The needle goes straight from 2 to 3. Think of this as one 2-3 stitch.

Carry the yarn backward to 4, then go from 4 straight through to the 1 directly below it on the chart. Think of this as a 4-1 stitch. This backward progression from 2-3 to 4-1 skips a row of holes. You can easily see the "skip" on the diagram; but it will be more difficult to see it on your canvas.

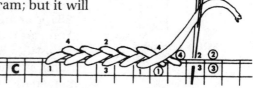

Binding Stitch #2

Practice until you feel confident. Now, fold your canvas so that Row B and two canvas threads are on top of the fold. Continue the same stitch progression this time pulling the yarn tight with each stitch. Note that when Row B is your fold line, Row A is at the back of your work, and Row C is at the front with the holes of these two rows perfectly aligned over one another. Also note that your needle is passing through Rows A and C simultaneously. After working an inch or two, open up the flap. It looks quite different because, by pulling your yarn tight, you have created a flat, neat braid and your edge will stay down.

Before you start binding a finished piece, trim all edges to 1 inch (or slightly less if you want less hem or turn-under). Then work as follows:

1. Turn the canvas so that the wrong side is facing you.
2. Row A is the last row of holes with stitches of the main design.

3. Fold the canvas so that Row B and two threads of canvas are on top of the fold. Row C is now facing you.

4. Secure your yarn in back of nearby stitches and come up at 1. Carry your yarn over the fold to 2-3. Backtrack to 4-1. Your needle is always coming straight toward you and the yarn is carried over the top of the fold. Do not let your tension get too loose. You do not want a floppy braid—pull a little tight.

5. When you run out of yarn, take the needle back at 2 and weave through the back of nearby stitches.

6. When approaching a corner, be sure that you have at least 6 inches to 8 inches of yarn in your needle to take you around the corner.

7. Before you get to the corner, you need to miter it. Fold the corner inward (a) so that one hole remains on the outside of the diagonal fold. Crease the adjacent sides as you did in Step 3 and refold the top edge (b). Holding all edges in as well as you can, continue around the corner, adding a few extra stitches to cover the "point." Once around the corner, you can pick up your regular stitch progression. When you reconnect with the beginning stitch, take a few extra stitches so that all threads are covered.

When you are using the binding stitch to join pieces, you need not consider any other trim as the binding stitch itself gives a finished edging. In many instances, linings will be desirable. See p. 28 for lining tips.

You can follow the general directions above for many items such as tote bags, belts, eyeglass cases, and the like, using the binding stitch for joining seams and finishing any open edges. It can even be used for assembling a pillow, although it is generally preferable to put a pillow together on the sewing machine as described below.

Although not absolutely necessary, you will probably want to use some type of cord, braid, or "gimp" for the pillow edges.

Any of the trims mentioned in the last paragraph can, of course, be purchased but you can easily make a round knitted cord using either your background yarn or one of the accent colors used in the piece.

You will need several uncut yards of the yarn to be used in the knitted cord. Because the yarn quantity will vary according to your needle size and yarn weight, I cannot give you an exact amount. I would suggest that you determine this by knitting an inch of cord with the needles and yarn you plan to use. Next, cut your yarn and rip out the stitches. Measure the amount of yarn used in making the 1 inch. Make note of this length and then decide how long a cord you will need. Multiply the 1-inch

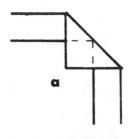

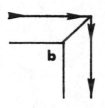

Miter Corners

requirement by the number of total inches you desire and you will have a good yardage guide.

Another good choice is a twisted cord. For most pillows, cut two to six strands approximately 8 to 12 yards long. The number of strands will determine the thickness of the cord.

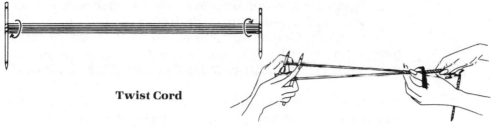

Twist Cord

Now call on a helpful neighbor, friend, or spouse. Tie one end of yarn strands around a pencil. Then loop the yarn over a second pencil held approximately 3 to 3½ yards from the first. (This is why you need a helper.) Now loop it over the first pencil, back over the second pencil, and back again to the first.

Each person now twists a pencil with one twisting clockwise and the other twisting counterclockwise, keeping the yarn taut. When the yarn begins to kink, let one person hold the center of the yarn while the other person holds both pencils. Gradually release the yarn, letting it twist naturally.

A knife-edge pillow is fairly simple to put together. In the beginning of this section, you were told to work a couple of extra rows of tent stitch around the outer edges of your piece.

1. When this has been done, it is then advisable to run a couple of rows of machine stitching along all edges just outside that double row of tent stitch (in the unworked margin) to prevent raveling.

2. Using the needlepoint piece as a guide, cut out a piece of backing fabric. You should have a seam allowance on your needlepoint piece so if the backing is cut to the same size, you will automatically have the necessary seam allowances on it.

3. At this point, you will need to decide if you want a bias cording stitched in between the needlepoint and the backing. If so, pin the cording to the right side of the needlepoint, realizing that your stitching line will be between the outer pillow stitches and the double row of tent stitches. For an inexperienced seamstress, I would recommend use of a cording that can be attached after joining, such as the knitted cord described previously, thus eliminating this last step.

4. Pin the two pieces together with wrong sides facing out. Next, baste them together so that your backing fabric will stay smoothly in place.

5. Now, with the needlepoint side facing up, machine stitch around three sides, making a neat, sharp turn at each corner and backstitching at the beginning and ending of these seams. Your stitching line is between the pillow stitches and the double row of tent stitches.

6. Trim your seam allowances about ¼ inch outside the double row of machine stitching made in Step 1.

7. Turn the pillow cover right side out, and insert the pillow form or Dacron polyester pillow stuffing, taking care to see that the stuffing is evenly distributed so that your finished pillow will be smooth.

8. Turn under the seam allowance on the needlepoint piece and backing on the remaining open edge and whip together by hand.

9. Whip any desired cording around edges.

For practice, why not make a little pincushion first? All of the same techniques will be used and you can learn if you do have the skills to successfully finish your own pillows. The pincushion will be a useful item that you can keep or give as a gift.

LINING Tote bags, eyeglass cases, belts, and many other items will require a lining. Such linings can be worked in one of two ways. These are described on p. 28 in the plastic canvas section. The same principles will apply.

PICTURES Mounting your own needlepoint pictures may be easier than you might think, particularly now that "self-stik" mounting boards are available in most needlework shops and at many notions counters. Full directions are included with these products so I will not go into those details here.

If you can't find these mounting boards, you can still do your own with a technique known as "lacing." You will need a firm board, cut to the exact measurements of your finished needlepoint.

Also, you should have an unworked margin of *at least* 2 inches around all edges of your canvas.

When you have blocked the canvas so that all edges are straight and all corners are square, you are ready to lace the canvas to the board. You will need some strong cord or twine—yarn, which has a certain amount of "give" or elasticity, is not a good choice for lacing.

Fold the unworked margin of canvas over the board, taping it in place here and there until you have done enough taping to hold it securely, mitering all corners.

Thread the cord into a large-eyed needle and insert the needle into the canvas about ½ inch in from the edge of the board at one of the corners. Pull the needle up so that all but about 2 inches of cord has been pulled through the canvas. Tie this end securely to the cord where it entered the canvas and you will be ready to lace.

Then take the needle across the back of the board and bring it through the canvas directly opposite the point where you started. Now, go back across the board and bring the needle up about 1 inch left or right of the first lacing stitch on that side. Go back to the other side and do the same thing.

Continue in this manner, taking some extra stitches in each corner. When you have it securely laced in one direction, do the same in the other. The main secret to success is to pull very firmly with each lacing stitch.

This is not your only choice, however. You can glue, staple, or tack the needlepoint to the mounting board, if you prefer.

PLASTIC CANVAS

Plastic canvas has actually been around for many years but it is only recently that is has really exploded on the needlepoint scene. Innovations are appearing so rapidly that there may be many new versions by the time this goes to print. **Categories**

To the best of my knowledge, it is presently available in three mesh sizes: 6-mesh, 7-mesh, and 10-mesh. It is most commonly found in 10½-inch-by-13-inch sheets, but the 7-mesh is also available in place-mat size rectangles and ovals and in pre-cut shapes (the latter often available only in kits). Both 7- and 10-mesh have been available by the yard, but I understand that this may be discontinued.

One of the newer innovations is color in 7-mesh and 10-mesh canvas. The colored canvas is a particularly good choice for the first-timer or for anyone with very limited time as no background filling is necessary. The first colors to be marketed were Christmas reds and greens, followed by soft pastels. Now you can find royal blue, brown, orange, and white with other colors certain to be added in the future.

"Stitch-a-Frame" is an ingenious idea featuring small round and rectangular plastic frames with the matching colored canvas molded to the frame so that you have ready-framed miniature pictures or coasters with absolutely no finishing required.

Some needlepoint purists frown on the use of plastic canvas and even feel that stitches worked on this material should not be called needlepoint at all. Many others feel that it is an exciting **Pros and Cons**

23

material, particularly good for newcomers to the craft. So let's talk about the pros and cons of plastic canvas.

It is a fairly stiff material so it is not really suitable for soft items such as pillows. This very stiffness, however, makes it ideally suited for projects such as tote bags, notebook covers, eyeglass cases, Christmas ornaments, and a wide variety of other gift and accessory items.

It won't warp out of shape no matter what stitch you use, so it is never necessary to do any blocking. I suppose that it is possible that someone could pull their stitches so tight that some buckling could occur, but I have never seen this happen, even with beginners.

Another reason for its popularity, even with experienced needle-pointers, is the ease of finishing. Many talented needle-pointers have to pay dearly to have their stitchery mounted or put together by professionals as an entirely different set of skills are required for finishing of traditional canvases.

You have no "raw" edges on plastic canvas and there is no need to turn under hems, miter corners, or use involved binding stitches. You simply cut the canvas so that there is one unworked rib, or thread, of the plastic around the outer edges of each piece. To cover unworked edges or to join pieces, just work a lacing, overcast, or binding stitch on the edges. (See finishing section.)

Selection of Stitches

Your choice of stitches for plastic canvas is very wide. Almost any slanting stitch can be used and most straight stitches, as well. In fact, I hesitate to make any exceptions as someone is sure to prove me wrong.

I do feel, however, that some stitches are not really practical and unless there is a very specific reason for using such stitches, why bother when there are so many others that work so well?

"Eye" stitches, where several stitches are to be taken in a single hole, can pose a problem unless you are using a fine yarn because the plastic canvas is rigid and does not "give" in the way that traditional canvas does.

Whether or not you get good coverage with long straight stitches on 7-mesh plastic will depend upon the yarn used and the way you handle it. If you are using worsted weight, try using double strands. This is one time you will have to be particularly careful not to let your yarn twist.

The 10-mesh is much more adaptable to straight stitches. When this size canvas originally was introduced, it had ridges that ran in one direction on one side and in the opposite direction on the other side. To successfully use straight stitches you had to take care to work over the ridges and not between them. Happily, this has been eliminated in the newer 10-mesh canvas with improved technology.

Another early problem—which has also been overcome in the better grades of plastic—was an uneven mesh count. This created difficulties when trying to make squares with the same number of stitches on all sides and when joining box shapes. I wrote several columns on this subject, always warning people to be sure and cut all pieces in the same direction so that the sides would match.

Both of the problems mentioned above still exist in some of the canvas on the market. The newer, improved type generally costs no more, so I would suggest that you be sure to get the best. To test for an even mesh count place one piece over another at right angles. You can then tell at a glance if the holes line up exactly over one another. If they do not, you know that the mesh count will vary horizontally and vertically. At least one brand has standard mesh count on all sheets, so that if you purchase sheets of this brand at different times or even from different sources, the mesh will match on all sheets—an important feature if you run short of canvas in the middle of a project.

To test for ridges, simply run your fingernail across the canvas first in one direction and then in the other. This will quickly tell you if there are more pronounced ridges in one direction. If you do find prominent ridges in one direction, this will alert you to the fact that you also probably have canvas with an uneven mesh count.

Yarn Choices

Synthetic knitting and crochet yarns have been the most common choice for use with plastic canvas—primarily the 4-ply knitted worsted weight. So that I will not be going into lengthy descriptions in the following paragraphs, let me define the terms I will be using. I will refer to the above mentioned yarn simply as worsted weight. Bulky yarn will refer to yarns of the size normally thought of as rug yarns, while sports yarn will identify a medium-weight yarn. Anything lighter will simply be called lightweight. Persian-type yarns are now available in acrylic fibers that are often excellent choices. (See the description of Persian yarn in the section on traditional canvas for tips on handling and using this kind of yarn.)

I am a firm believer that there is no one right yarn for any particular canvas, although obviously some work better than others. The guidelines I will give you are simply suggestions. Experiment to your heart's delight and use whatever suits you.

6-MESH CANVAS Probably the reason that this size is less popular than the 7-mesh is because it is more of a problem to find a suitable yarn. Bulky-type yarn is often the best choice. One of my favorites is Bernat Tabriz—a 100 percent polyester with a pleasing sheen. The only problem here is that a fairly large needle is needed with this yarn and some people find it difficult to pull the needle through, particularly where several stitches share a hole. A loosely twisted knitting worsted will sometimes cover sufficiently if great care is taken to keep a loose, even tension. Double strands of knitting worsted will work, as will multiple strands of Persian yarn, but this can make your project much more expensive. Wool rug yarn is the easiest to handle, but again, this can become expensive. In my opinion, you are much better off with 7-mesh.

7-MESH CANVAS For tent stitches and many pattern stitches, a single strand of worsted-weight yarn works extremely well, with double strands used for Bargello. The only drawback here is that it is seldom found in less that 3½-ounce skeins, which is fine when you need a large amount, but is wasteful when only a yard or two is needed. I will often use if for the large areas and then use four or five plies of Persian-type acrylic yarn for the accent areas. In addition, there are new nylon, Herculon, and polyester yarns being marketed specifically for needlepoint in a worsted weight. Most of these have a slight sheen, a hard surface that is dirt-resistant, and have the added advantage of no "pilling." Best of all, some are being marketed in small skeins at a very reasonable price.

10-MESH CANVAS My favorite for this canvas is Persian-type yarn, used with two or three plies in the needle, depending on the stitch used. The brand of yarn can determine the number of plies as well, as I find some thicker than others. Some worsted-weight yarns work well, but some are too heavy for easy stitching—and who wants to be pulling and tugging at needlepoint? On the colored 10-mesh, where complete coverage is not the idea, I have successfully used sports weight and even finer for scattered pattern stitches, achieving an open, airy effect that I find quite pleasing.

Bargello patterns work exceedingly well on 10-mesh, particulary those with an even-mesh count—you can even successfully work four-way Bargello. Persian-type is particularly good but light worsted weight is also very suitable. For really nice pieces, I use the wool Persians for some elegant effects and even embroidery floss for some lace-like designs.

In general, as for traditional canvas, don't limit yourself in your choice of yarns. Raffia, jute, ribbon, and other materials can make an outstanding creation. Just let your imagination go and remember: Needlepoint should be fun!

Once your stitching is completed, finishing your plastic canvas project is simpler than you might imagine. First, be sure that all outer edges are smooth—trim away any little nubs that might be protruding.

Finishing and Cleaning

FINISHING In most cases a simple overcast or lacing stitch is used for joining the various pieces and for edging all unfinished edges. To do this: (1) Bring the needle up in an edge hole from the back of the work to the front of the work; (2) Take the needle to the back again and bring it up in the next hole. Keep repeating Step #2 all along the edge to be covered, taking extra stitches as needed in the corners—usually three stitches are needed to cover the corners.

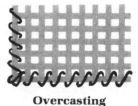

Overcasting

When two pieces are to be joined, work in the same manner, but hold the two together with wrong sides together and right sides facing out. When joining, you will be working through matching holes of each piece, thus joining and finishing at the same time.

An alternate finishing stitch is the picot edging. To do this: (1) Bring the needle up in the second hole from one corner; (2) Take the yarn to the back of the work and bring the needle up in the corner hole; (3) Skip over these two stitches and one empty hole, then bring the needle up in the next hole; (4) Bring the needle up in the skipped hole. Repeat Steps #3 and #4 across, taking extra stitches, as needed, to cover corners. This may be used for finishing unworked edges or for joining pieces.

For the more experienced needlepointer, the binding stitch described on p. 18-20 in the section on finishing traditional canvas is an excellent choice for many projects.

Usually you will be given specific construction tips for the order in which you should put the various pieces together for the specific project you are making. But if not, here are some good general rules to follow.

When putting together any box-like shapes, I find it best to first join each side piece to the bottom piece. Then, I join each side piece to the neighboring side piece, *always* working from bottom to top. There is a logical reason for this. If you work from top to bottom, you will find it much more difficult to secure your yarn ends. If you were making something like a tissue box cover with a top attached but no bottom piece, you would do the reverse. In other words, always work *away* from the closed end.

When working with colored plastic canvas, I often do all finishing with a yarn as close to the color of the canvas as possible unless I want defined joining lines. When using the same color yarn, I sometimes overcast quickly by going into every other hole and taking no special care to cover the corners.

LINING If a lining is desired, you have two choices. If you are handy with the sewing machine, you can assemble the lining by machine, whipping the top edges of the lining to the top edge of the purse or other item to be lined. Or, if like many needlepointers, you prefer hand finishing, you have that option also. In either case, cut the lining pieces about 1 inch wider and 1 inch longer than each canvas piece. Then turn under a ½-inch seam allowance all around and press in place. For hand assembly, lay each piece on the wrong side of the corresponding needlepoint piece and whip in place with sewing thread as close to the color of the yarn as possible. Whip the lining close to the edge stitches, but do not let it extend beyond these stitches or it will be in your way when you are joining the pieces.

When selecting your lining fabric, be sure to select a permanent press type so that it will never require ironing when washed. The heat of the iron could ruin your project.

CLEANING PLASTIC CANVAS Heat is really the only thing you must avoid. Logically, you would assume that plastic canvas and acrylic yarns are machine washable but unless you are very certain that your washing machine truly has a reliable cool or cold water setting and a very gentle cycle, I would suggest that you wash them by hand. Sometimes a machine may have a cold water setting, but if the water pressure from the hot water tank is greater than the cold water pressure, the water may be too warm. To wash by hand, use cool water and a mild detergent, swishing the article around in the suds and again in the rinse water. If something is heavily soiled, you might want to let it soak for a while.

I do not recommend the use of a dryer in any circumstances as the heat from this appliance can warp the canvas. Nor should you dry the article in direct sunlight as some yarns will definitely fade in prolonged bright sunlight. By the way, while white may not fade as colors do, it will take on a yellow hue under the same conditions that cause color fading.

With the treatment recommended above, it really doesn't matter if you use wool or synthetic yarns. The wool will react favorably, as well.

Stitch Charts

The following diagrams show you the direction or slant of needlepoint stitches and the number of threads and holes over which each stitch passes.

The solid chart lines represent the threads (or ribs) of the canvas and the blank squares represent the holes of the canvas. There are two general numbering systems used. (1) The needle is brought up in odd numbered holes and taken down in even numbered holes. Example: Bring the needle up at #1, take it down to #2; up at #3, down at #4; up at #5 and down at #6 and so on. (2) Arrows are used and numbers may appear only where the needle comes up from the wrong to the right side of the work with arrow points showing you where the needle goes down into the canvas. A number in braces—(1) or (2)—after a stitch name will indicate the numbering system used. If any other system is used, instructions for following the specific chart will be given.

TENT STITCHES

The basic needlepoint stitch is the tent stitch. It is a single stitch diagonally crossing one mesh of the canvas. There are three primary ways to work the tent stitch, each appearing much the same on the front (or right side) of the canvas, but looking quite different on the back. If you take a quick glance at the following charts for two versions of this stitch—half-cross and continental—you might think they are worked in an identical manner.

But take another look. While the stitches themselves lay in the same direction, the numbers tell you that your working direction is different for each. In the half-cross, you are working from left to right, while in the continental, you are working from right to left. When you work each stitch following the chart, you will see that the continental pads the back of your work much more than the other does. This illustrates the importance of the numbering systems used in stitch charts.

Now, look at the basketweave stitch chart. As you can see, this is worked diagonally rather than horizontally or vertically, and it is crucial to follow the number sequence exactly as shown. This stitch also covers the canvas quite well.

Half-Cross Stitch

1. HALF-CROSS STITCH (2) The first row is worked from LEFT to RIGHT as shown by Steps (1-4). Continue across the row in the same manner until the desired number of stitches are worked. The next row below can be worked by starting just below the last stitch worked as shown in Step (5) and continuing back across in this manner as shown in Steps (5-8). Or, you can start over at the LEFT edge and work succeeding rows exactly as you did in Row 1. If you wish to work this stitch vertically, turn the chart sideways to see the vertical sequence of stitches.

Continental Stitch

2. CONTINENTAL STITCH (2) The first row is worked from RIGHT to LEFT as shown by Steps (1-4). Continue across the row in the same manner until the desired number of stitches are worked. The next row below can be worked by starting just below the last stitch worked as shown in Step (5) and continuing back across in this manner as shown in Steps (5-8). Or, you can start over at the RIGHT edge and work succeeding rows exactly as you did in Row 1. If you wish to work this stitch vertically, turn the chart sideways to see the vertical sequence of stitches.

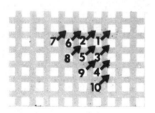

Basketweave Stitch

3. BASKETWEAVE (2) A very satisfactory version of the tent stitch for all but the first-time needlepointer. Once you establish the pattern of working back and forth diagonally there is never the problem of where to start succeeding rows.

Any of the tent stitches are suitable on any type of canvas and are used for design areas or background filling. They allow more detail than many pattern stitches.

Yarn requirements: The half-cross takes the least amount of yarn; in fact if directions furnished in a commercial kit specify this stitch, you should definitely use it as there will probably not be enough included for either of the others. For example: On 10-mesh canvas, 10 yards of yarn will cover approximately $9\frac{1}{2}$ square inches with half-cross, $6\frac{1}{2}$ square inches with continental, 6 square inches with basketweave.

Distortion of canvas: On traditional canvas, there can be a great deal of distortion with half-cross, somewhat less with continental, and the least amount of distortion with basketweave.

DECORATIVE STITCHES

Any of the stitches that follow can be considered "decorative." Many are easy enough for the beginning needlepointer. In fact, when teaching first-time needlepointers, I often start with one or more of the first several stitches shown before teaching the various tent stitches. This allows the beginner to see quick results and encourages them to try other decorative, or pattern, stitches. The stitches are arranged according to degree of difficulty—or perhaps I should say degree of simplicity—with the easiest stitches first.

The stitches included in this section are by no means all of the pattern stitches suitable for needlepoint. There are literally hundreds of pattern stitches, and I hope that I will simply whet your appetite for learning more. These will keep you busy for quite a while and allow you to add a great deal of excitement to your stitchery.

I suggest that you start a stitch notebook. Make samples of any or all of the stitches and place them in plastic sheet protectors in your loose-leaf notebook. Then when you start a new project, refer to your notebook for stitch selection.

This is perhaps a good time to bring up the subject of counting threads of canvas or holes of canvas when working pattern stitches. It is easier to count holes than to count threads, but there is a very good reason for doing the opposite. When you are trying to determine how many repeats of a pattern stitch will fit into a certain area, a hole count will give you the wrong information. Why? Look at your practice stitches. As you can see, each stitch shares holes with its neighbor. Every full pattern stitch, however, always covers the same number of threads, so do get into the habit of counting over threads instead of over holes.

Let's take an example to show you how to figure if a row of pattern stitches will fit into the given area. Suppose you have a canvas 48 threads wide and 66 threads deep and you want a Scotch-stitch border. A four-thread pattern requires a multiple of four threads; a three-thread pattern requires a multiple of three. Are the numbers divisible by four? One is and one is not, but both are divisible by three. In this case, the three-thread Scotch would be the logical choice. If you definitely want a four-thread Scotch-stitch border, you could adjust by working a single

31

row of tent stitches at the top and bottom reducing the vertical thread count to 64, which is divisible by four.

Beginner-Level Stitches The following stitches can easily be understood by even the needlepoint novice.

4. MOSAIC STITCH (1) The smaller chart shows two completed mosaic stitches. Starting near the upper right corner, follow the numbers from 1 to 6. At this point, you have completed one full mosaic stitch. Work in same manner from #7 through #12 for the second one. This will show you how two pattern stitches share the same holes at certain points. To start a second row, count down to the second empty hole below the place where you started your first stitch on Row 1, and bring the needle up in that hole and follow the same sequence as before.

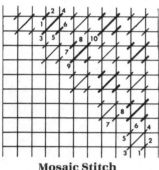

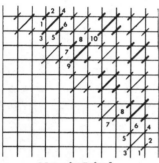

This stitch can be worked horizontally or vertically in either direction. It can also be worked diagonally as shown in the larger chart. To follow this chart, start near the top left corner and follow the numbers from 1 through 10. Complete this row following the bold lines down to the bottom of the canvas. Start the second row where #1 appears at the lower right of the chart from #1 through #8. Continue up this row, following the lighter lines to the top of the chart.

Mosaic Stitch

NOTE: The center—or longer—stitch in the mosaic stitch pattern is called a slanting Gobelin stitch. A slanting Gobelin stitch always crosses two or more threads diagonally. You will find this term used in several places in later stitch descriptions.

Scotch Stitch

5. SCOTCH STITCH (1) If you have mastered the mosaic stitch, you will find the Scotch stitch quite easy as it is simply a "grown-up" mosaic. Two charts are shown for this stitch, with the first covering four threads of canvas in each direction and the second covering only three threads.

Experiment with a two-color Scotch-stitch border, changing colors after each full Scotch stitch.

As with the mosaic stitch, this can be worked horizontally, vertically, or diagonally. When working diagonally, progress down the canvas in the same way you did for the mosaic stitch. If you work one diagonal row with one color and the adjoining row with another, alternating the colors in this manner every row, you will have a checked design.

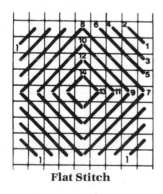

Flat Stitch

6. FLAT STITCH (1) This is simply a block of four Scotch stitches worked in alternating directions. After working from #1 through #14, start each following Scotch stitch as points marked

Flower Stitch

with #1. This is considered an intermediate-level stitch, best used as an accent stitch, although it can be an interesting background for certain projects. Try placing a French knot in the center of each flat stitch for special effect.

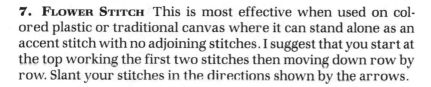

Basic Cross-Stitch

7. FLOWER STITCH This is most effective when used on colored plastic or traditional canvas where it can stand alone as an accent stitch with no adjoining stitches. I suggest that you start at the top working the first two stitches then moving down row by row. Slant your stitches in the directions shown by the arrows.

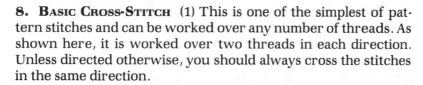

Elongated Cross-Stitch

8. BASIC CROSS-STITCH (1) This is one of the simplest of pattern stitches and can be worked over any number of threads. As shown here, it is worked over two threads in each direction. Unless directed otherwise, you should always cross the stitches in the same direction.

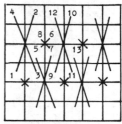

Double Cross-Stitch

9. ELONGATED CROSS-STITCH—TIED (1) In this version, you are crossing three threads vertically and two threads horizontally, making the stitch taller. Finish with a straight stitch from #5 to #6.

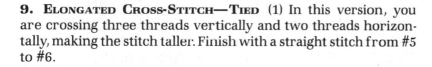

Upright Cross-Stitch

10. DOUBLE CROSS-STITCH (1) This is a combination of elongated and short cross-stitches, in staggered rows. Unless you want an open, airy effect, you might need extra strands of yarn for the long crosses to get good coverage.

11. UPRIGHT CROSS-STITCH (1) This cross-stitch is worked with two straight stitches, one vertical and the other horizontal. Follow the numbers on the chart as before. It also can be worked over any number of canvas threads.

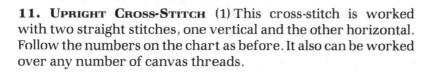

Smyrna Stitch

12. SMYRNA STITCH (2) If you have mastered the previous stitches 9 and 11, this one will be a snap! It is simply a combination of the two, but makes an outstanding decorative stitch. Follow the numbers as before and you will see that you start with a basic cross-stitch covered with an upright cross-stitch.

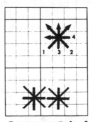

Smyrna Diamond

13. SMYRNA DIAMOND (1) The chart for this stitch appears very similar to that for the plain Smyrna. However, the stitch sequence and the stitch lengths are not the same and the effect is quite different. This is best as an accent stitch.

14. RICE STITCH (1) Another easy stitch, also started with a basic cross-stitch. After the basic cross is made, each of the

Rice Stitch

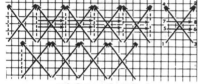

Rick Rack Stitch

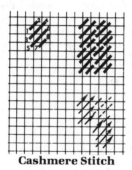

Cashmere Stitch

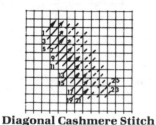

Diagonal Cashmere Stitch

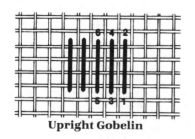

Upright Gobelin

corners is crossed, starting with #5 on the chart, work Steps 5-6, then Steps 7-8. The next chart shows Steps 9 through 12. This stitch is most effective worked in two colors, using one color for Steps 1-4 and another for the remaining steps. For ease in working, do all of the cross-stitches first and then cross the corners after completing the cross-stitches. This stitch is also known as William & Mary stitch or crossed corners.

15. RICK RACK STITCH (1) This stitch starts with an irregular cross-stitch, covering four threads horizontally and five threads vertically—(Steps 1-2-3-4). Next, two straight stitches are made over the center of the cross—(Steps 5-6-7-8). Notice that the second row is staggered below the first. Row 3 would be like Row 1 and Row 4 would be like Row 2. After a row is completed, work the vertical straight stitches that are shown by broken lines in a contrast color. This is an open stitch that allows the canvas to show and is best suited for colored canvas.

16. CASHMERE STITCH (1) This can be worked vertically, horizontally, or diagonally. A single cashmere stitch is shown with the stitch sequence numbered. The block of stitches shown by bold lines shows how stitches join each other when worked in horizontal or vertical rows. Finally, the chart with arrows and broken lines illustrates how this stitch is worked diagonally.

17. DIAGONAL CASHMERE STITCH (2) Don't be fooled—this is not the same as the straight cashmere stitch worked diagonally. Try both and you will see that the effect is quite different. For this stitch, bring the needle up in a numbered hole and take it down at the tip of the arrow leading from that number. Work in sequence, starting at #1 and progressing through #2, #3, #4, and so on. An excellent stitch for a textured background. Suitable for any type of canvas.

18. UPRIGHT GOBELIN (1) This is one of many staight stitches. It is to the "family of straight stitches"—including Bargello or Florentine work—what the tent stitches are to the "family of slanted stitches." That is, it is the basic straight stitch. Often in a piece worked overall in this stitch, chart symbols will represent a block of four stitches. For an example of this, see the Master of the Hunt Wallhanging on p. 70-72. Working in the manner shown in the chart, will cover the canvas back and front. You could use less yarn by working the first stitch from the bottom to the top and the next stitch from the top to the bottom, but your stitches would not lay flat and smooth if you did so. It is also exceedingly important to keep your yarn flat, particularly when using Persian-type yarn, as discussed in the section on yarns.

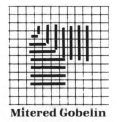

Mitered Gobelin

19. MITERED GOBELIN Upright Gobelin makes a very effective border—easy enough for the beginner. If you are unaccustomed to figuring spacing for borders, you will probably find it easiest to start at one corner with a single stitch over just one canvas thread. Move over one hole to the right and make a stitch over two threads; move over one more and make a stitch over three threads; move over yet one more and make a stitch over four threads. Continue across in a straight line to the other corner. Note how stitches abut in the corners.

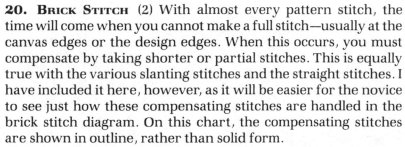

Brick Stitch

20. BRICK STITCH (2) With almost every pattern stitch, the time will come when you cannot make a full stitch—usually at the canvas edges or the design edges. When this occurs, you must compensate by taking shorter or partial stitches. This is equally true with the various slanting stitches and the straight stitches. I have included it here, however, as it will be easier for the novice to see just how these compensating stitches are handled in the brick stitch diagram. On this chart, the compensating stitches are shown in outline, rather than solid form.

This stitch can be worked in one of two ways—horizontally, as shown, or diagonally. Notice that Row 1, shown by numbered bold arrows, is worked from right to left, skipping every other hole. Row 2, shown by the thin arrows, is then worked from left to right in the skipped spaces. The third row is shown by braces. When working diagonally, start at the upper left corner and work down to the lower right corner for Row 1. Turn the canvas upside down to work Row 2. While the horizontal version is easier for the beginner, it takes a bit more yarn than the diagonal version.

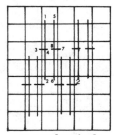

French Stitch

21. FRENCH STITCH (1) Without the horizontal stitches, this would be called a "double" brick stitch. To make it a French stitch, these little short tie-down horizontal stitches are worked as you go. Follow the numbering sequence carefully.

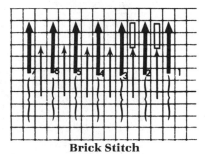

22. HUNGARIAN STITCH (1) Consisting of short and long straight stitches, this is an excellent background stitch, lending an interesting texture without overpowering the design. Notice that you take one short, one long, and one short stitch for one Hungarian stitch; skip one hole and make another. Succeeding rows may be a bit tricky for the beginner, so pay close attention to the chart until you become familiar with the stitch sequence.

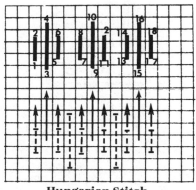

Hungarian Stitch

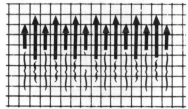

Parisian Stitch

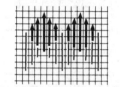

Bargello Diamonds #1

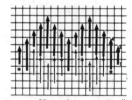

Bargello Diamonds #2

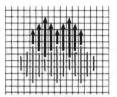

Bargello Diamonds #3

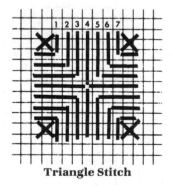

Triangle Stitch

A second row is shown in the lower part of the chart by broken lines.

23. PARISIAN STITCH At first glance, this may appear to be identical to the Hungarian, and while it is quite similar, the effect is different. By working them both on the same practice piece of canvas, the differences in stitch sequence and the final appearance will be apparent.

24, 25, 26. BARGELLO DIAMONDS These diamonds can be worked in a variety of ways. The first pattern is perhaps the easiest. Start at either side and work across following the bold arrows. Then work another row immediately below, following the narrow lines. This second row can be worked in the same or a contrasting color.

The second pattern is very similar, but a space is left between each diamond. As you will see, the long stitch of each diamond on the second row fits into this space.

A more advanced version of a Bargello diamond is shown in Chart #3. To start this, count down nine holes from the top and two holes over from the right edge, bringing the needle up in that hole (#1 on the chart) and taking it down at #2. Working from right to left, for the first row, bring the needle up at the base of each bold arrow and take it down at the tip of the same arrow. To repeat across a full row, repeat the steps from * to *. The second row is worked by following the lighter arrows.

27. TRIANGLE STITCH (2) This is another interesting pattern of straight stitches that can be varied in many ways. Each square block consists of four triangles. Follow Steps 1 through 7 for the first triangle, then work around the square clockwise. Fill in the corners with cross-stitches. Or, if you have adjoining blocks of triangle stitches, you will end up with four-thread squares between the blocks, and you have a choice of several different pattern stitches to use in those spaces. Try working the vertical stitches in one color and the horizontal stitches in another or even work each triangle in a different color. You can have a lot of fun experimenting with various color arrangements.

28. GATHERING STITCH (1) This is worked much like a Bargello diamond through Step 10. At that point, use your left thumbnail to pull the long center stitch to the side and bring the needle up in the center hole (shown by the black dot to the left of the center stitch). Working on top of the canvas, pass the needle under the two stitches to the left of the center. Bring it over the top of all the stitches, then pass it under the two stitches to the right of the center. Take the needle down through the same hole under the center stitch as shown by the other black dot, pulling the yarn firmly to "gather." A variation of this stitch, known as the wheat stitch or wheat sheaf stitch is worked in the same manner, having all vertical stitches of the same length.

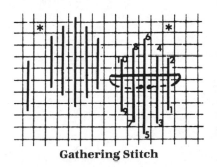

Gathering Stitch

29. BASIC BARGELLO There are dozens of variations of Bargello or Florentine stitches, traditionally worked in softly blending shades of one or two colors. Today, we often see these same stitch patterns using boldly contrasting colors. While these patterns might appear quite complicated, most are very simple once the "base line" is established as most are simply repeats of the same line of stitches over and over. The following chart is a good basic pattern using curves and short and long peaks.

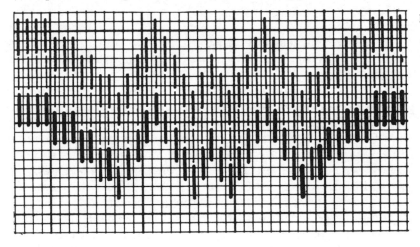

Basic Bargello

(While I had stressed earlier that it was better to count by threads rather than holes, I am more often referring to hole count in introducing these stitches as it is usually easier for the beginner when learning.)

Count carefully for your first row, because a mistake made in this row will be repeated in each succeeding row. Mark the canvas for the upper right corner. Count down to the fifth hole from the corner and bring the needle up in that hole. Count up over four threads (or three holes) and take the needle down in the hole above. Move over one hole from the base of the first stitch and bring the needle up; take the needle down one hole to the left of the top of the first stitch. Make two more stitches in the same manner. You have now completed the first block of four stitches in the upper right corner.

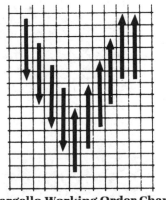

Bargello Working Order Chart

Now, move over one hole to the left and two holes down from the base of the last stitch made. Again count up four threads and take the needle now in the next hole. Repeat twice more. Reading from right to left, you have made the first seven stitches of the top row. Continue across to the top left corner, taking one stitch for each vertical line on the chart. When the first row is complete, work a second row directly under it in the same manner with a different color. Work the entire piece in this way changing color for each row.

To have all the stitches padded equally on the back of the work, start a stitch at the botton when moving down a Bargello line and start from the top when moving up a Bargello line. See the Bargello Working Order Chart.

There are other versions of the Bargello stitch among the needlepoint projects featured in the next chapter. See p. 51, 57, 121.

Intermediate-Level Stitches

If you have successfully mastered a few of the preceding stitches, now's the time to try some really fascinating decorative stitches.

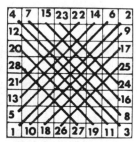

7-Thread Waffle Stitch

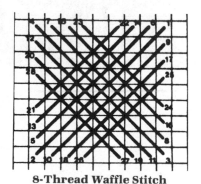

8-Thread Waffle Stitch

30. WAFFLE STITCH The first few times you try this, you will probably be glued to the chart for each step. After a while, though, you will see the logic of each progression and should be able to work without the chart. Two separate charts are shown. One is worked over a square of seven canvas threads and is started in the lower right corner. The other is worked over an eight-thread square and begins at the upper right.

For practice, begin with the eight-thread chart. Bring your needle up in the hole at the upper right corner. With the tip of your needle, count down diagonally across eight threads or mesh of the canvas. This is the trickiest part, but is very important. If you have difficulty counting accurately on the diagonal, count straight down across eight threads (from #1 to #3 on the chart) and then horizontally across eight threads (from #3 to #2 on the chart). At this point, take the needle down from the right to the wrong side. This completes Steps 1-2. Next, count across from left to right over eight threads and bring the needle up at #3 on the chart. Now, count up diagonally across eight threads to #4 on the chart and take the needle down at this point. Next, bring the needle up in the hole just above Step 2 where #5 appears on the chart. Just to the left of #1 you will find #6. The needle goes down at this point.

Continue following the numbers in order, always bringing the needle up at odd numbers and taking it down at even numbers.

When you come to the last step (27-28), pass the needle under the diagonal thread formed by Steps 21-22 before taking it down at #28. All of this sounds very complicated, but I think you will find it relatively easy if you take it one step at a time. It is best used as an accent stitch. This does not adapt well to compensating stitches so use only with the correct multiple of threads.

This stitch does not cover the back of your work well, so if you plan to have other stitches above, below, or to the side of one or more waffle stitch, work them first, so that you will have a good place to secure your yarn.

31. DIAMOND WAFFLE (1) For special effect, try the diamond waffle. At the widest point in each direction, this stitch covers 10 canvas threads. The stitch lines are not shown on this chart as they tend to make the chart more complicated to follow, and careful counting of the canvas threads is critical to successful completion of this stitch. Bring the needle up at #1, lay the yarn smoothly across the canvas, and take the needle down into the canvas hole at #2. Follow the numerical progression. The diamond waffle is recommended as an accent stitch.

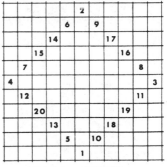

Diamond Waffle

32. DOUBLE LEVIATHAN STITCH (1) This is another excellent accent stitch although it can be used as an overall geometric pattern whenever you have a multiple of four threads. Start by making a four-thread basic cross-stitch (Steps 1-4). Then follow the chart numbers, in sequence, as shown. The stitch is charted in three stages so that you may check your progress at each stage.

Double Leviathan Stitch

33. RHODES STITCH (1) This looks quite similar to the previous stitch, but there are definite differences. It is worked over a six-thread square and the progression or sequence of stitches is different. Follow this chart as with the previous ones by bringing the needle up at odd numbers and taking the needle down at even numbers. This is another stitch best used as an accent.

Rhodes Stitch

34. MILANESE STITCH (2) Worked in a solid color, this is a beautiful textured background stitch. Worked in alternating rows of contrast color, it is a stunning overall pattern for pillows, purses, and many other items. Work one diagonal row, starting at #1 and progressing down from left to right, following the bold lines. An adjoining row is shown in finer lines. To work the second row, turn the chart and canvas upside down and begin with the first light line in the lower right corner.

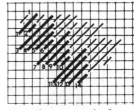

Milanese Stitch

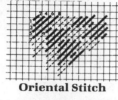

Oriental Stitch

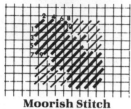

Moorish Stitch

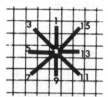

Algerian Eye or Square Eyelet

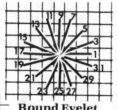

Round Eyelet or Daisy Stitch

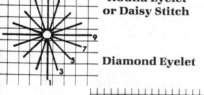

Diamond Eyelet

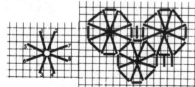

Octagonal Eye or Pinwheel Stitch

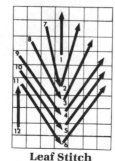

Leaf Stitch

35. ORIENTAL STITCH (1) This is very similar to the Milanese stitch except that rows of slanting Gobelin stitches (shown by the broken lines on the chart) are worked between each repeat of the main pattern.

36. MOORISH STITCH (1) The central pattern is shown in solid lines and is worked diagonally from the top left corner down, following the numerical sequence shown. Slanting Gobelin stitches (shown by the lighter lines) are worked on either side of each main pattern repeat.

37. ALGERIAN EYE OR SQUARE EYELET (2) This stitch and the following three stitches are all versions of the eyelet stitch. The base of all versions of the eyelet is a center hole into which the needle is taken down for each stitch. These stitches are not very suitable for plastic canvas and work best on woven mono as several stitches are taken in one hole. With the woven mono, you can enlarge the center hole before starting by inserting the tip of a knitting needle or a large tapestry needle into the hole and rotating it several times. If you wish to use these stitches on plastic canvas, you should probably use finer yarn than normal as you cannot enlarge the holes satisfactorily.

For the Algerian eye, follow the numbers counterclockwise; bring the needle up in the odd numbered holes; cross two canvas threads; and take the needle down in the center hole.

38. ROUND EYELET OR DAISY STITCH (2) Stitches 5, 13, 21, and 29 cover two canvas threads, while all others cover three canvas threads.

39. DIAMOND EYELET (2) Stitch #1 covers four threads, stitch #3 covers three threads, stitch #5 covers two threads, stitch #7 covers three threads. This is a beautiful accent stitch when using the right type of canvas.

40. OCTAGONAL EYE OR PINWHEEL STITCH (2) All stitches of the octagonal eye cover three canvas threads. Start at #1 and work around clockwise in numerical sequence. Then work back stitches all around each octagon as shown.

41. LEAF STITCH (2) This stitch is extremely effective but requires careful counting. In the chart, each number indicates the point where the needle is brought up through the canvas. The needle is taken down at the tip of each arrow. Work Steps 1 through 6, moving down the canvas, then go up to the top of the leaf and work down for Steps 7 through 11, thus completing one leaf stitch. To make a second leaf stitch diagonally below and to the left, bring the needle up at #12 on the chart, thus making the first stitch of the second leaf. Work the second leaf in the same order as before.

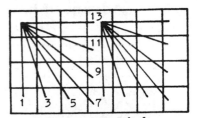
Ray or Fan Stitch

42. RAY OR FAN STITCH (2) Like the eyelet stitches, all of the individual stitches end in a single hole. This is highly effective as a corner stitch in a stitch sampler, although it can be used as an overall pattern. The chart shows how the stitches are made side by side.

43. JACQUARD This is composed of a series of slanting Gobelin stitches as shown by the bold arrows, bordered on both sides by single tent stitches, which are shown as open ovals on the chart. While this can be worked in any direction—and the direction is often determined by the area to be covered—try starting in the upper right corner on a practice piece. The tent stitches can be worked in the same or a contrasting color. Or you might want to work all tent stitches in one color and alternate a variety of colors for the Gobelin stitches.

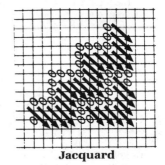
Jacquard

44. STEM STITCH (2) This is usually worked in vertical rows and makes an excellent border. Work Steps 1 through 11, then make a row of backstitches as shown by the solid straight lines, starting at the top and working down. This is a very small sample of the stitch. In actually working, you would first make all of the stitches to the left of the center, from top to bottom, and then work your way up the opposite side of the center from bottom to top.

Stem Stitch

45. FISHBONE STITCH (1) The main portion of this stitch (Steps 1-2 and 5-6) is shown worked over four canvas threads. It can be worked over as few as two or as many as eight. The short "tie-down" stitches (Steps 3-4 and 7-8) are always worked over a single mesh. The working order is the same as for the stem stitch.

Fishbone Stitch

46. 8-POINT STAR OR CANTERBURY CROSS (2) A highly effective stitch used singly or in groups. The wavy lines show how a second Canterbury cross adjoins the first. When you have a group of four crosses, you will have an eight-thread space in the center into which you can fit a flat stitch, an eight-thread waffle, or any number of other stitches. As an example of this, see the Tissue Box Covers pattern on p. 102-104.

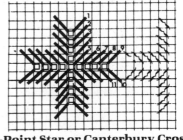
8-Point Star or Canterbury Cross

Advanced-Level Stitches These remaining stitches are for the more experienced needlepointer.

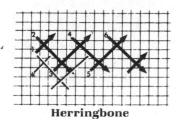

Herringbone

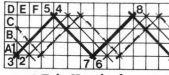

6-Trip Herringbone or Bazaar Stitch

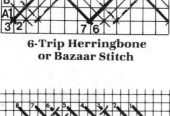

Diagonal Weave

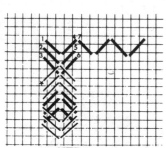

Perspective Stitch

47. HERRINGBONE (1) This is a fascinating stitch and is particularly effective as a two-color border. Follow the stitch progression in Row 1 from #1 through #7. The seventh stitch shows how to end a row, but you can repeat the fifth and sixth stitches all across until you near the right-hand edge, at which time you will take the seventh stitch. The start of the second row is designated by an asterisk (*).

48. 6-TRIP HERRINGBONE OR BAZAAR STITCH (1) Careful counting is necessary for this stitch. There are several versions of it, but the one shown can be worked in six colors for an outstanding border stitch. Start with color A at #1, continue with it across the row, following the numerical sequence. Color B stitches are shown by the lighter lines and Color C by the dashed lines. Remaining colors are worked in the same manner, with starting point for each color designated by a letter on the chart.

49. DIAGONAL WEAVE Start in the upper right corner and work all the stitches shown by bold arrows first. If you wish to cover a larger area than the one shown, continue across the top of the canvas for as many stitches as desired instead of turning the corner for Stitch 9 as shown. After all of these long stitches are finished, use a contrasting color to work the groups of three shorter diagonal stitches over the top of the others. The very short stitches shown are compensating stitches that will always be needed at the edges of the pattern. Wherever possible, however, make the full group of three four-thread stitches.

50. PERSPECTIVE STITCH This is worked in horizontal rows, with each row consisting of several groups of the first six stitches shown. In other words, for Row 1, work Steps 1 through 6 first. Then moving to the right, work the additional groups of the same six steps (see #7 on the top row for the start of the second group). When this row is completed, with a contrasting color, start a second row at the point marked with a star on the chart—again working a horizontal row. Continuing to alternate dark and light colors, follow the chart through the third and fourth horizontal rows.

51. ROCOCO STITCH (1) For really dramatic effects, this stitch is hard to top. Bring the needle up at #1. Keeping the yarn slack, take the needle down at #2. Now, to make the "tie-down" stitch, bring it up at #3 and, passing over the slack yarn, take it down at #4. With a little practice, you will be able to judge the correct tension. Steps 5 and 6 use the same holes as #1 and #2, again keeping the yarn slack. Make another "tie-down" as before (Steps 7-8). This completes the right side of the stitch. Complete the second half—or left side—of the stitch in the same manner. One example of this stitch in use can be seen in the Merry Christmas Ornaments pattern on p. 141-145.

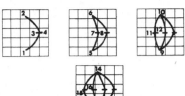

Rococo Stitch

52. PETAL STITCH Work the first petal by following the thread count and stitch progression from #1 through #5. (Stitch #1 covers five diagonal threads.) Work the other three petals in the same manner. Then, holding the stitches aside with your left thumb nail, bring the needle up at the point shown by the small arrow. Next, weave the yarn under the petals (working on top of the canvas) in a counterclockwise motion. Continue round and round, keeping each coil flat, until the area under the petals is filled. Finally, make one small "tie-down" stitch over the outer coil at the points where an "o" appears on the chart.

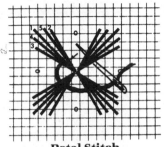

Petal Stitch

53. WOVEN SPIDER WEB STITCH First, make seven spokes, radiating from a center hole as shown by the straight diagonal lines. Then bring the needle up in an empty hole adjacent to the center hole. Now, working on top of the canvas, *weave over spoke 1, under spoke 2, over spoke 3, under #4, over #5, under #6, over #7, under #1, over #2, under #3, over #4, under #5, over #6, under #7.* Repeat steps from * to * until the area is full of coils. This looks surprisingly like a rose in full bloom when completed.

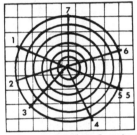

Woven Spiderweb Stitch

54. FRENCH KNOT After bringing the needle up through the canvas at #1, wrap the yarn once around the needle. With your left thumb and forefinger, hold the yarn taut to the left of the needle while you take the needle down at #2. Continue to hold the yarn securely until all the yarn is pulled through. A cluster of French knots makes a beautiful flower center.

French Knot

55. TURKEY WORK This stitch is quite unique in that it gives you a fluffy pile. Try it for flower centers, Santa beards, bunny tails—or anywhere you want a fluffy texture. For these very special effects, experiment with this stitch, always starting with the bottom row and working up.

To begin, you do NOT secure your yarn on the wrong side. Just let it hang free on the right side. (The beginning of the strand is designated by an asterisk on the chart.) Then, take the

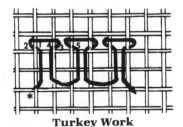

Turkey Work

needle *down* at #1 and bring it *up* at #2. Go across two threads and take the needle down at #3 and bring it up at #4.

Before starting the second stitch at #5, let a loop hang free below the row you are working. It helps to hold this loop in position with your left thumb as you start the second stitch. Work across from left to right for as many stitches as needed to cover the area. At the end of the row, cut the yarn, letting the free end hang at the front of the work. The succeeding rows are worked above the base row.

When all stitches are completed, cut all the loops and trim them to the desired height. The final step is to "worry" the stitches. To do this, with the tip of a sharp needle, rub back and forth over the cut pile to fluff it up. Or you might try using a fine tooth comb for this.

Needlepoint Projects

WATERFORD DIAMOND PILLOW

MATERIALS

One 18-by-18-inch square of six-to-the-inch double-thread 100 percent cotton canvas

#16 tapestry needle

22 skeins (8.8 yards per skein) Bernat Tabriz Needle Art yarn, Color 5873

½-yard fabric for backing

One 14-inch pillow form

A word before you begin: Please read the directions completely—step by step, all the way to the end—before you begin your stitching. That way, you will know from the very start just how everything will come together, stitch by stitch and detail by detail, to produce the beautiful work you want.

GENERAL HINTS

1. The long stitches might cause your canvas to pucker. To avoid this, work your quick-stitch on a stretcher frame that can be purchased from any large art supply store.
2. Cut yarn to no longer than 24-inch lengths for best working results.
3. Do not tie any knots.
4. To start first stitch, leave about 1 inch of yarn on wrong side, being sure to work over this end as you progress.
5. Work, stitching evenly, being sure to ease the yarn comfortably through the canvas—never pulling too tightly or stitching too loosely.
6. To finish off yarn, run needle under a few stitches on wrong side near stopping point. Clip yarn close to canvas.

Blocking: Your finished piece is not likely to be out of shape. But if that happens, just dampen back of work and, while it is damp, thumbtack it down all around. Let it dry in place. Then dampen again and press with a warm iron (not a hot iron) on the wrong side. Do not wash—dry clean only.

Finishing Pillow: Trim canvas ½ inch from worked area. Cut backing same size as trimmed canvas. Place right sides of canvas and lining together. Machine-stitch on three sides being sure to stitch close to worked edge so canvas will not show. Clip corners for ease in turning and turn right side out. Insert pillow form or stuff with desired filling. After turning in raw edges, sew remaining seam by hand. If you wish to insert zipper, purchase proper size and follow manufacturer's instructions.

To Begin Pattern

1. Measure in and make a small pencil line 8 inches in and 8 inches down from upper left corner of canvas (see Corner Mark Diagram).
2. Each grid line on the charts represents a canvas thread.
3. The letter in each area on Chart A shows the stitch to use to fill in the area.
4. Come up at (●) and down at (X) to work first stitch in each area on Chart A.
5. Come up at odd numbers and go down at even numbers on stitch diagrams.
6. Start at corner mark and following Stitch Diagram A1 work a square, starting at number 1. Fill in square by following Stitch Diagram A2. Matching stitch diagrams to Chart A, fill in remaining areas of pillow. Turn canvas to work around center square as indicated by arrows on Chart A.

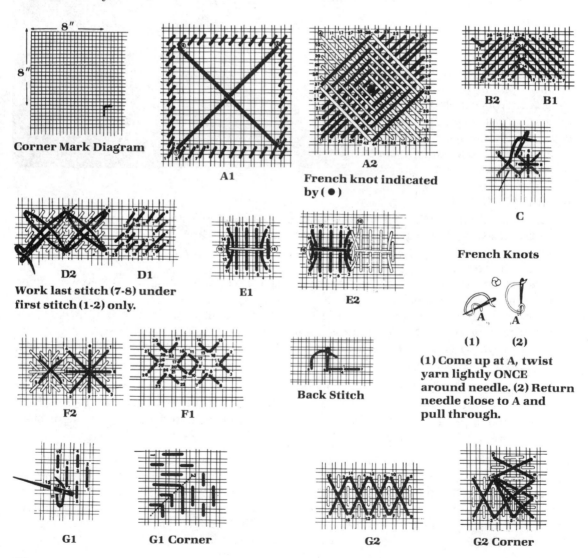

Corner Mark Diagram

A1

A2

French knot indicated by (●)

B2   **B1**

C

French Knots

D2   **D1**

Work last stitch (7-8) under first stitch (1-2) only.

E1

E2

Back Stitch

(1)   **(2)**

(1) Come up at A, twist yarn lightly ONCE around needle. (2) Return needle close to A and pull through.

F2   **F1**

G1   **G1 Corner**   **G2**   **G2 Corner**

48

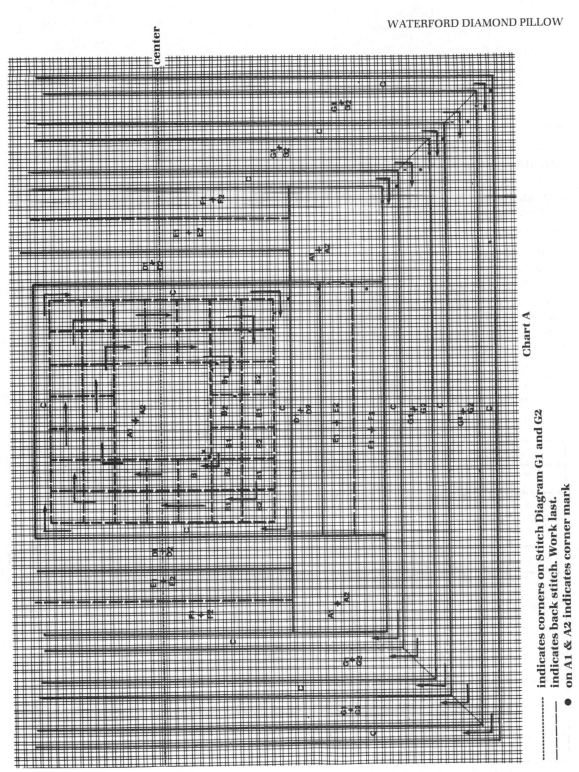

center

Chart A

------------- indicates corners on Stitch Diagram G1 and G2

─ ─ ─ ─ indicates back stitch. Work last.

──────── on A1 & A2 indicates corner mark

● indicates corner mark

49

STITCHING TIPS

Some of the charts for this project are a bit difficult to follow, so I am including some clarifications to make them easier for you.

Stitch Chart D1 shows the base—or setup—for the finished pattern stitch. You first make a series of adjoining tent stitch "boxes."

Stitch Chart D2 shows you how the top cross lies on top of these boxes. In the Clarification Chart, you will find the same thing charted in a different manner. To start the overlay, bring needle up at base of arrow at the point designated by a * on Chart D1—this is the same place as shown by #1 on Chart D2. Take needle down at #2. Continue in this manner, bringing needle up at odd numbers and taking it down at even numbers, keeping in sequence of numbers. Notice that stitch 7-8 passes over stitch 5-6 and under stitch 1-2.

Chart G2 for corner: The first Chart G2 gives you a better idea of how the finished stitch appears than does the Clarification Chart. However, it is most difficult to read the numbers and letters that give you the sequence of the stitches, so I have outlined it, leaving off the stitch lines. The dotted lines on the Clarification Chart represent the base stitches that are also shown in Chart G1. These should be worked first. The numbers 1 and 2 that I have inserted on the G1 chart show you the starting point for the overlay stitches. To follow Clarification Chart G2, work as before, bringing needle up at #1 and taking it down at #2. Continue in this manner through #10. Then bring needle up at A, down at B; up at C, down at D; up at E, down at F; up at G, down at H; up at I, down at J; up at K, down at L. When you finish with Stitch K-L, the corner is complete.

Clarification Chart

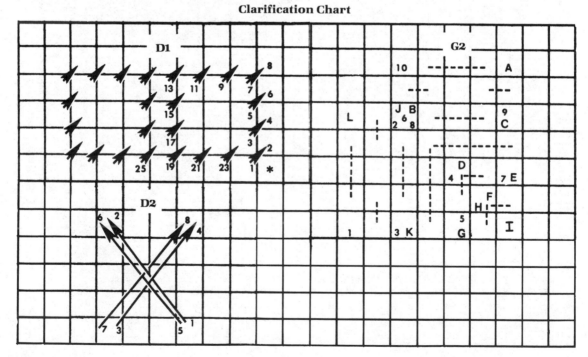

PAIR OF BARGELLO PILLOWS

MATERIALS

Brunsana Persian yarn or any Persian or tapestry yarn of your choice: one skein each color (color numbers given in instructions are for Brunsana)

For either style pillow: One 18-inch square of 12-mesh interlock canvas
One 14-by-14-inch pillow form
#20 tapestry needle
One 40-yard skein Persian or tapestry yarn in each color
½-yard fabric of your choice for pillow backing

The finished size of each pillow front should be 14-by-14 square inches. You are instructed to start with an 18-inch square of canvas. This allows for a 2-inch unworked margin all around. Tape all edges with masking tape before starting.

To find exact center of canvas, fold canvas in half lengthwise and run a basting thread along the center fold. Open canvas out and fold in half in the other direction and again baste along the center fold. Where the two basting threads cross will be the center of your canvas.

It is important that you secure all loose yarn ends as you go. These ends are secured by running them through the back of previously worked stitches. In Bargello work, it is suggested that you first run the needle through the backs of stitches in one direction and then pass it under several stitches in the opposite direction so that the loose ends will not work loose. When you finish with one strand of yarn and pass it under stitches, immediately clip off the remaining yarn. Leaving loose ends can cause tangles and knots that may later show on the right side of your work. When you start your design, you will, of course, have no stitches in which to secure the loose end. So, knot the end of the first strand of yarn; pass the needle through from right side to wrong side about six inches from center of canvas; after taking several stitches, cut knot and run loose end under these stitches.

The secret to ease in following seemingly complicated Bargello patterns lies in establishing the "base lines" and centering the design accurately. Once the basic motif or base line is established, the remaining lines of stitches usually fall into place quite easily.

In some Bargello patterns you will find stitches of varying lengths. In each of these two designs, however, the stitch length remains the same throughout. For Pillow A, each stitch covers four threads of the canvas. For Pillow B, each stitch covers six threads of canvas.

Each line on the charts represents one thread of the canvas, while each square on the charts represents one hole in the canvas. The symbols within each stitch outline represent the color to be used for that stitch. Color codes are given for each under the specific instructions for each pillow.

PILLOW A: Suggested Color Combinations

blue tones	green tones	brown-beige tones	coral-russet tones
106 royal blue	416 dark bayberry	235 coffee	394 dark papaya
108 robin blue	415 bayberry	266 mocha	372 paprika
56 sky blue	414 medium bayberry	181 caramel	393 papaya
97 schooner blue	413 light bayberry	74 cream caramel	392 medium papaya
68 baby blue	227 pale sea foam	43 pale beige	391 light papaya

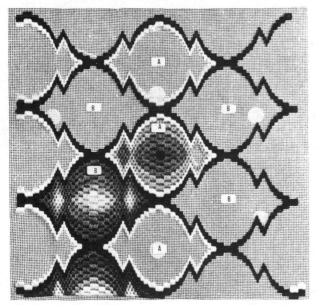

PILLOW A
(shown at left in photograph)

Medallion "A" Color Code		Medallion "B" Color Code
darkest color		lightest color
medium dark		lightest color
medium color		medium light
medium light		medium
lightest color		medium dark

Both "A" and "B" medallions are outlined in the darkest color—

Both "A" and "B" medallions are worked alike EXCEPT for the color sequence.

All stitches in this design are taken over four threads of canvas. In other words, bring needle up in one hole, count up over four threads and take needle down in next hole above. When your stitch line moves up (Step Up 2), count two threads below top of last stitch, bring needle up in hole below second thread, count up four threads and take needle down in next hole above. When your stitch line moves down (Step Down 2), count two threads below base of last stitch, bring needle up in hole below second thread, count up four threads and take needle down in next hole above.

Find exact center of canvas. Count down two threads below center and two threads to right of center; bring needle up at this point; count up over four threads and take needle down in hole above fourth thread. Working from right to left, make four more stitches in exactly same way. You have now completed the stitches marked with ⬭⬭⬭⬭⬭ on chart. Continue to work out from center, following color codes. Complete this medallion by outlining it in darkest color as shown by the stitch symbols marked:⬭⬭⬭⬭⬭. Now, work all of the medallion outlines as shown, filling in medallions after outlines are completed.

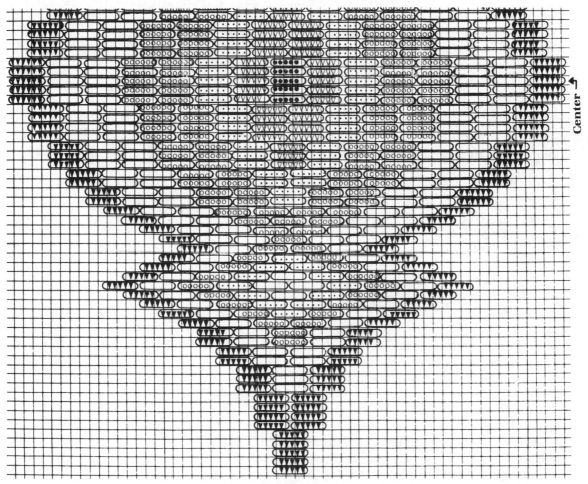

Chart for Pillow A Shown at Left in Photograph

PILLOW B: Suggested Color Combinations

blue tones		green tones		brown-beige tones		coral-russet tones
Same as Pillow A except eliminate schooner blue	I	Same as Pillow A except eliminate light bayberry	I	Same as Pillow A except eliminate cream caramel	I	Same as Pillow A except eliminate medium papaya
PLUS		PLUS		PLUS		PLUS
229 medium tiger	II	229 medium tiger	II	393 papaya	II	388 nude
164 light tiger		164 light tiger		392 medium papaya		387 au natural
232 pale tiger		232 pale tiger		391 light papaya		386 buff
PLUS		PLUS		PLUS		PLUS
* 83 magenta	III	* 83 magenta	III	*119 deep melon	III	*119 deep melon
*416 dark bayberry		*416 dark bayberry		*416 dark bayberry		*416 dark bayberry
** 84 deep pink		** 84 deep pink		**122 light melon		**122 light melon
**126 light rose		**126 light rose		**210 pale melon		**210 pale melon

  *For colors marked with single asterisk, you will need one yard.
 **For colors marked with double asterisk, you will need three yards.
   For all other colors, you will need a 40-yard skein.

PILLOW B
(shown at right in photograph)

There are three separate color groups for this design. Color Group I is used for the basic stripes around the medallions. Color Group II is used for the diamond shaped medallions. Color Group III is used to make the rose design in the middle of the center medallions.

Color Code for Group I:

(▲▲▲▲▲) darkest color
(♦♦♦♦♦) medium color
(△△△△△) light color
(⬭) palest color

Color Code for Group II:

(●●●●●) dark color
(○○○○○) medium color
····· light color

Color Code for Group III:

♦ dark bayberry green
X magenta or deep melon
* deep pink or light melon
o light rose or pale melon

Tent Stitch

Find and mark the exact center of canvas. Thread needle with Color * from Group III. You will find one * on the chart with a circle around it. This is the stitch to be taken in the exact center of canvas. The rose design is worked in tent stitch, as illustrated. Each symbol in this section of chart represents one stitch made in color denoted by that symbol.

    When you have completed the rose design, thread needle with palest color from Group I. Count down eight threads below the bottom stitch of rose design (♦) and bring needle up in hole just below the eighth thread. This will be at point A on chart. This first Bargello (or straight) stitch to be taken is also marked with this symbol: . Count up over six threads and take needle down in hole just above the sixth thread. Now make another stitch in same manner to the left of the first stitch. Make two more stitches in same manner. Now—in the next hole to the left—count up three threads, bring needle up, count up over

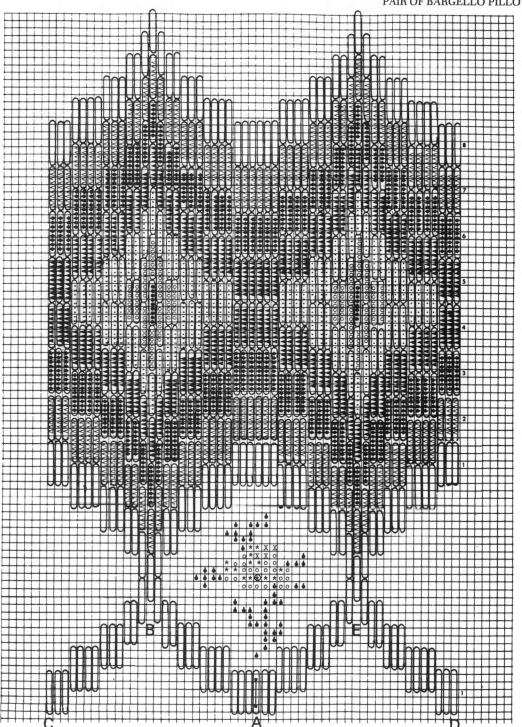

Chart for Pillow B Shown at Right in Photograph

six threads, and take needle down. You have made the first of a group of four stitches to the left of center group of six stitches.

NOTE: All Bargello stitches in this design are made over six threads of canvas. (This is the same as working over five holes if you prefer to count that way.) When your stitch line moves up or down, you always move up or down three threads above or below the previous stitch.

Now, continue to follow chart from A to B; then work from B to C. When you have completed Stitch C, continue stitching toward the left edge of canvas, but move to Stitch D on chart. When you finish Stitch D and the two identical stitches next to it, you will have six stitches side by side. Now follow chart from D to E to A to B to C, then repeat from D to E once more. You will now have the bottom half of two and a half medallions. When this is done, start again at the center and make two stitches to the right of first stitch made at A. This time working toward right edge, work from A to E to D to C to B to A. Continue in this manner until you reach the bottom line of five medallions across. Now, turn chart upside down and work other side of the five medallions (or top of medallions).

Next, starting at either side edge, work row of stitches in light color from Group I (Row 2 on chart). Work Row 3 with medium color; Row 4 with dark color; Row 5 with dark color; Row 6 medium; Row 7 light; Row 8 palest color. Fill in the diamond shaped medallions, starting with light color, then with medium color, and ending with one dark color stitch in center. Turn pillow and chart around and work bottom half of pillow to correspond to top half. Use palest color to work tent stitch background in each rose medallion. Fill in unfinished semicircles at top and bottom with Bargello in darkest color.

BARGELLO RIBBONS PILLOW

MATERIALS

#20 tapestry needles, pillow form, cording, and fabric for backing

14-mesh mono canvas: Canvas should be cut 2 inches larger on all four sides than desired finished measurements of pillow. For example, purchase a 14-inch square of canvas for a 10-by-10-inch pillow or a 16 square inch for a 12-by-12-inch pillow.

Yarn: You may use 40-yard skeins of tapestry yarn or 2-ply Persian yarn. The model pillow was worked with four shades of green (Colors A, B, C, D) and four tones from pink to red (Colors E, F, G, H) for the ribbons, with black (Color X) used in the centers. One skein of each of the nine colors was used.

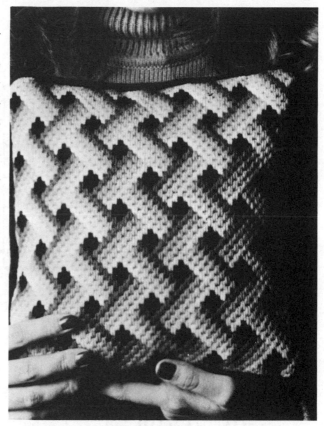

Look at the Actual Stitch Diagram. You will see that each "stair step" consists of two side-by-side stitches. Each stitch is worked over four canvas threads. Each lettered block on the Working Diagram represents one block of these two side-by-side stitches worked in the color designated by the letter.

To begin, mark the area to be covered with pattern with sewing thread and long basting stitches, leaving a 2-inch margin outside the markings on all edges. To establish the pattern, I suggest that you start with the diagonal row of paired stitches marked on the Working Diagram with eight "Ds." Start at the base of the bottom "D," coming in 13 holes from the right side marking and up 10 holes from the bottom edge marking.

IMPORTANT: EACH LETTER IN WORKING DIAGRAM REPRESENTS TWO SIDE-BY-SIDE STITCHES.

After working the line of D stitches, change to another color tone and work the line of C stitches; change color again and work the line of B stitches, followed by a line of A stitches. Next, work the four pairs of stitches marked with Xs. Then, changing colors as before, work lines H, G, F, and E in that order. This establishes your color and pattern sequence, making it easy to follow the balance of the pattern. Work in any direction you please, stopping the pattern at your thread markings at each edge.

Working Diagram

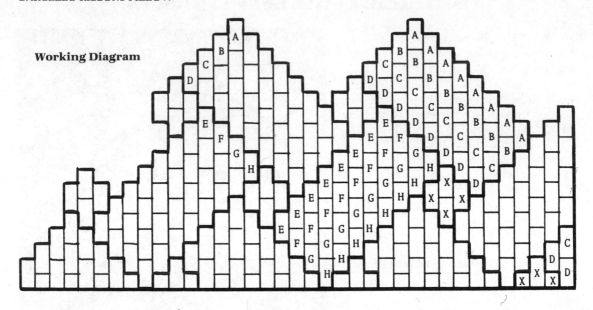

Actual Stitch Diagram

| = A

‡ = B

| = C

‡ = D

BOX DESIGN PILLOW

MATERIALS

Mono needlepoint canvas with 10-mesh to the inch—purchase a 15-by-15-inch square

Tapestry yarn: You will need two 40-yard skeins of the color you select for outlining the blocks and for the border. You will also need two skeins for colors selected for Y and X sections of chart. (See stitch and color key.) For the other colors, one skein of each color will be sufficient.

Pillow form, 7-inch zipper, and ½-yard fabric for pillow back, box sides, and cording

You may use any color combination you desire. The model pillow was made in brown and orange tones and colors mentioned here are those actually used.

For ease in working, make all of the outlines of the squares first, using orange (or the color of your choice). Then you should work in the letters of your choice in the squares labeled "A" on the chart. The letters are designed to be worked in cross-stitch, with the background worked in tent stitch.

All of the unmarked sections are to be worked in slanting Gobelin. You alternate colors Y and X as shown in the upper left section of main chart.

Stitch and Color Key

A— Letter squares: Letters are cross-stitched in brown; tent stitch background in light coral.
B— Tent stitch worked in medium coral.
C— Scotch or Scottish stitch squares with horizontal and vertical bars separating the Scotch stitch squares giving the "window pane" effect.
C-1— Bars worked in copper; Scotch stitch in beige.
C-2— Bars worked in medium coral; Scotch stitch in copper.
C-3— Bars worked in copper; Scotch stitch in light coral.
C-4— Bars worked in medium coral; Scotch stitch in light rust.
C-5— Bars worked in light rust; Scotch stitch in medium coral.
C-6— Bars worked in orange; Scotch stitch in medium coral.
C-7— Bars worked in beige; Scotch stitch in copper.
C-8— Bars worked in light rust; Scotch stitch in beige.
C-9— Bars worked in beige; Scotch stitch in brown.
C-10— Bars worked in brown; Scotch stitch in light rust.
D— Diagonal stripe: Work two rows of brown and two rows of beige alternately, starting in upper lefthand corner.
E— Smyrna stitch: E-1 is worked with the cross-stitch in brown and the upright cross in beige. Reverse the colors for E-2.

BOX DESIGN PILLOW

F— Tweed stitch: Starting in upper lefthand corner, using the diagonal or basketweave stitch, alternate rows of beige, medium coral, and light rust.

G— Work as for F with medium coral, light coral, and copper.

H— Diagonal mosaic worked in beige.

X and Y— Slanting Gobelin stitch. X is beige; Y is brown.

NOTE: In the small, unmarked rectangles found on each side of the pillow chart, use any color and any stitch that you like.

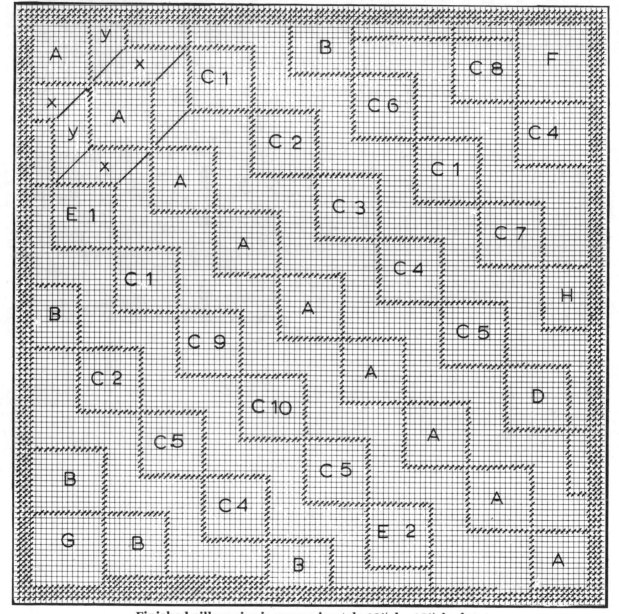

Finished pillow size is approximately 10½-by-10½ inches.

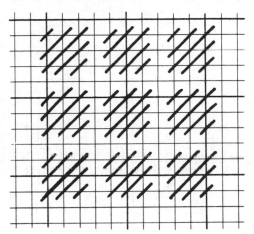
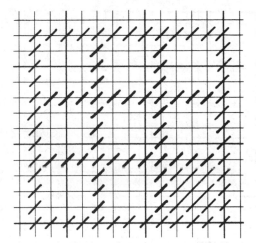

Scotch (or Scottish) Stitch: This stitch combines diagonal satin stitch with tent stitch. Start with a tent stitch first, then go over two meshes with next stitch, over three meshes, over two meshes, ending with a tent stitch over one mesh. Leave one canvas thread, vertically and horizontally, between each square of Scotch stitch. Fill this space in later with contrasting color in tent stitch. This is referred to as the bar in the stitch and color key.

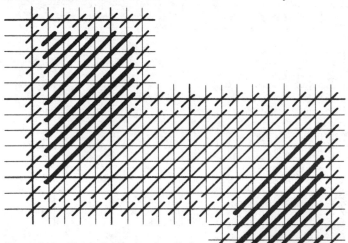

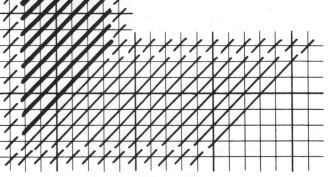

Slanting Gobelin Stitch: Each stitch covers six meshes of the canvas. Bold lines denote Color X; lighter lines denote Color Y. Note that compensating stitches must be used to fill in at each end of canvas.

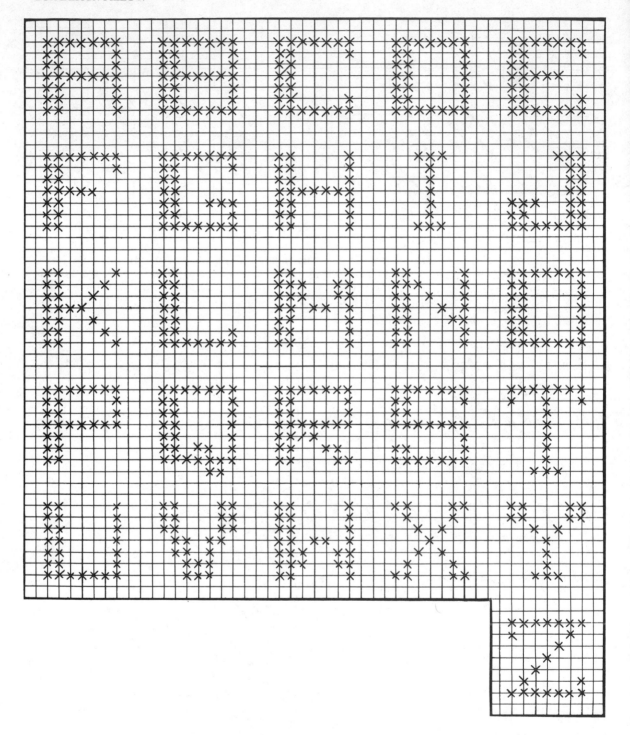

SAMPLER PILLOW

MATERIALS

16-inch square of single-thread tapestry canvas (mono), 10 meshes per inch

Yarn: 80 yards of tapestry yarn in Color A (off white or pastel shade); 40 yards of Color B (medium light); 80 yards of Color C (medium dark); 120 yards of Color D (darkest shade); 3 yards of Color E (metallic thread)

#18 tapestry needle

16-inch-square piece of medium-weight fabric in matching color for back of pillow

13-inch-square pillow form

To Begin: Bind all edges of canvas with masking tape to prevent raveling. Mark the top of your canvas with an X on the masking tape and always remember to hold your canvas top-up when working the stitches. Begin in the center of the design. Find the center of your canvas by folding it in half horizontally and then in half vertically. Work the large cross—straight cross (#1) and then do the diagonal mosaic stitches (#2) until all diamonds are completed. Fill in these diamonds with the stitches indicated. In reading the graph, note that the number indicates the type of stitch, all of which are illustrated here, and the letter indicates the color. In following the stitch charts, always bring your needle up on the odd number (1-3-5) and down on the even number (2-4-6). Always use this up-and-down motion rather than a sewing motion.

If you are using Persian-type tapestry yarn (recommended), be aware that one strand consists of three thin strands loosely twisted together. In the following instructions, one strand means one triple strand; two strands means to use two triple strands. For best results, first separate the triple strands and then place them back together side by side. Use one strand of yarn except when doing the following stitches: (#1) Use two strands for the large cross and one for the straight cross. Use two strands for each of the following: (#3) diamond stitch; (#7) Bargello; (#9) rice stitch; (#10) double stitch larger crosses (use single strand for smaller crosses); (#12) long legged cross; (#13) Parisian stitch. When you have completed your design, there will be a few areas of canvas that show. Cover them with tent stitches. Where the ray stitch meets in the corner with the diagonal mosaic, there will not be room to complete an additional row of ray, so complete with tent stitch in Color B. Work two rows of tent stitch around the entire design.

Finishing: If necessary, the needlepoint may be blocked in the following manner: Place needlepoint on a well-padded board, with right side up. Using rust-proof pins, stretch canvas to shape and pin to board. Wet piece thoroughly. Allow to dry completely before removing it from board. Cut away excess canvas, leaving a ¾-inch seam allowance. With

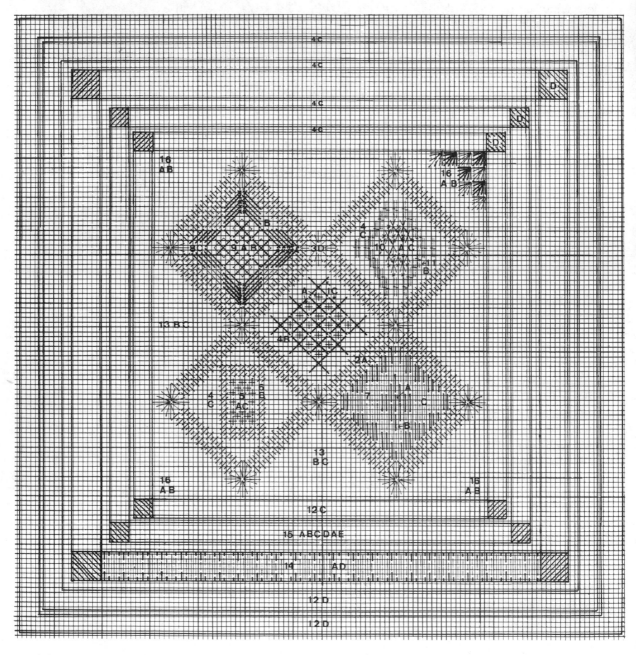

right sides facing each other, baste and sew canvas and fabric backing together along three sides. Work with the needlepoint side facing you, taking care to have the two-stitch border in the seam allowance. Turn to right side, insert pillow form, turn under seam allowance, and slipstitch closed.

Color Key

COLOR A— very light or off white
COLOR B— medium light
COLOR C— medium dark
COLOR D—darkest shade
COLOR E— metallic thread

Stitch Key

1. Large cross—straight cross
2. Diagonal mosaic or Florence
3. Diamond eyelet
4. Tent—half-cross
5. Straight cross
6. Cashmere
7. Florentine or Bargello
8. Modified fishbone
9. Rice
10. Double stitch or double cross
11. French
12. Long-legged cross
13. Parisian
14. Diamond
15. Herringbone
16. Ray or fan

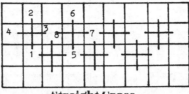
Straight Cross

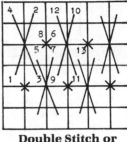
Double Stitch or Double Cross

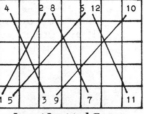
Long-Legged Cross

Tent—Half-Cross

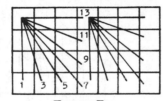

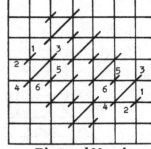
Diagonal Mosaic or Florence

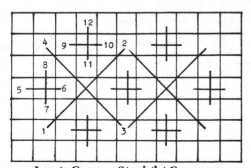
Ray or Fan

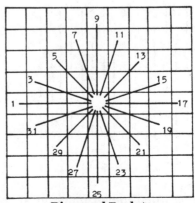

Large Cross—Straight Cross or Double Cross Stitch
Always work the large cross first.

Diamond Eyelet (even numbers at center)

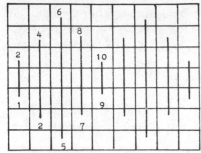

Diamond

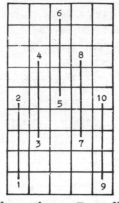

Florentine or Bargello
Basic pattern is over
four threads and up two.

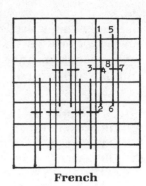

French

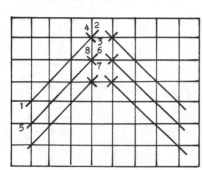

Modified Fishbone

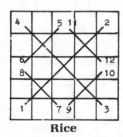

Rice

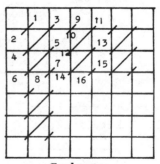

Herringbone
(Continue, using six progressions in varying colors.)

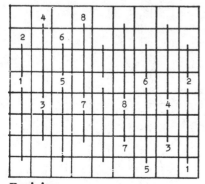

Parisian
(The long stitch comes under the short stitch.)

Cashmere

ROW HOUSE WALL HANGING (OR RUG)

MATERIALS

Coats & Clark's Craft & Rug Yarn, 3-ply (4-ounce pull-out skeins):

No. 111 eggshell	2 skeins
No. 902 jockey red	60 yards
No. 668 lime green	60 yards
No. 740 atomic pink	45 yards
No. 403 gray	30 yards
No. 360 wood brown	30 yards
No. 243 mid orange	30 yards
No. 253 tangerine	30 yards
No. 676 emerald green	30 yards
No. 12 black	30 yards
No. 848 skipper blue	30 yards
No. 230 yellow	15 yards
No. 764 deep purple	15 yards

Rug or tapestry needle with eye large enough to thread rug yarn into it

32-by-44-inch piece of canvas, five meshes to the inch

For rug: 4 yards of rug binding, 1½ inches wide; rug backing

For wall hanging: plywood for mounting

Tape all edges of canvas with masking tape to prevent raveling while working. Mark the center of canvas in each direction (horizontally and vertically) with a line of basting stitches. You will note that there are arrows at the bottom and at the right-hand edges of the chart showing the center meshes. Starting at center of canvas where basting stitches cross and following chart, work in colors as follows:

Background: eggshell
Front Lawn: lime green
All Window Panes: gray
Trunks of Trees and Shrubs: wood brown
Leaves of Trees and Shrubs: emerald green
House No. 1— Walls: mid-orange. Roof and Chimney: wood brown. Roof Tiles: yellow. Attic Window (outer frame): yellow. All Shutters, Window Frames, and Door Frame: wood brown. Door: jockey red. Window Box Flowers: lime green and jockey red
House No. 2— Walls: atomic pink. Roof Tiles and Chimney: deep purple. Window Frames and Stoop: deep purple. Door: skipper blue. Window Box Flowers: lime green and tangerine
House No. 3— Walls: jockey red. Roof and Chimney: black. Roof Tiles: jockey red. Window Frames and Door: black
House No. 4— Walls: tangerine. Roof and Chimney: skipper blue. Roof Tiles: yellow. Window and Door Frames: skipper blue. Door: yellow. Plant Pots and Flowers on Shrubs: yellow. Window Box Flowers: lime green and yellow

Work in continental stitch, using 1-yard lengths of yarn throughout. Be careful not to pull yarn too tightly in order not to distort the canvas. If canvas does distort, block it as follows: Place canvas wrong-side-up on a well-padded board. Using rustproof pins, pin to board along edges, stretching to correct shape as you pin. Wet canvas thoroughly and leave pinned to board until completely dry. Machine-stitch around edge of work about four times to keep it from raveling.

Finishing of Rug: Sew one edge of binding to right side of canvas around entire outer edge, bordering edges of design. Trim canvas. Turn binding to wrong side and sew in place. Sew backing to wrong side of rug.

Finishing of Wall Hanging: Mount canvas on plywood. Frame, if desired.

Center Mesh

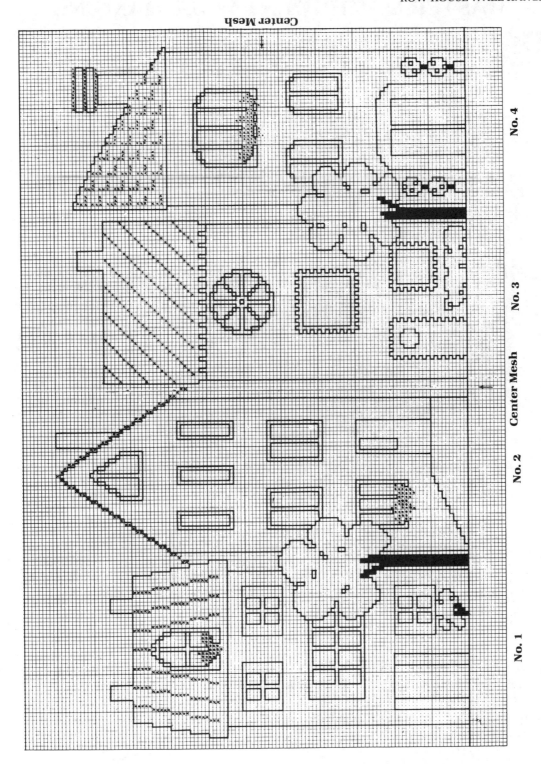

No. 4

No. 3

Center Mesh

No. 2

No. 1

MASTER OF THE HUNT WALL HANGING

MATERIALS

Coats & Clark's Red Heart Needlepoint and Crewel Yarn:

  nineteen skeins blue jewel #355
  four skeins olive #510
*seven skeins forest green #507
  three skeins white #011
  three skeins blue-violet #640
  three skeins tan #466
  two skeins light purple #653
  two skeins mid purple #643
  two skeins baby blue #756
  one skein fawn beige #132
  one skein dark gray #180

#18 or #20 tapestry needle

Single-thread tapestry canvas, 18-mesh (18 threads per inch), one piece 27-by-23 inches

¾-yard of medium-weight fabric, 36 inches wide for backing

Wooden rod or cane approximately 27 inches long and ¾ inches diameter

*only three skeins of forest green are needed for the needlepoint design. The extra four skeins are for making tassels and cording. Purchased tassels and cording can be substituted if desired.

Mark center of canvas both ways with a line of basting stitches. The chart shown gives complete design with the exception of six rows above the chart that are to be worked in background color (blue jewel). EACH SQUARE ON THE CHART REPRESENTS ONE BLOCK OF FOUR STRAIGHT OR SATIN STITCHES, each worked over four threads of canvas (see Stitch Block Chart). To work this simple stitch, bring needle up at #1, take it down at #2, bring it up at #3, take it down at #4, bring it up at #5, take it down at #6, bring it up at #7, and take it down at #8, thus completing a block of four stitches.

The center of the design is indicated by the blank arrows that should match basting lines. Start design at center, following chart by taking one block of four stitches for every symbol on chart. Use Color Code to identify symbols.

Stitch Block Chart

Finishing: Trim canvas to within 1 inch of stitches. Trim backing fabric to same size. With right sides together, stitch fabric to canvas close to needlepoint stitches on sides and lower edge, leaving 1½ inches free at top of side. Turn to right side. To make a channel for rod, turn in seam allowance on top edges and slipstitch together. Insert rod. Attach cord and a tassel at each end of rod.

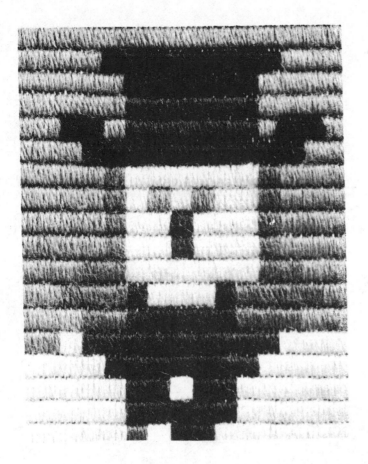

Color Code:

◰ —653 light purple

☒ —643 mid purple

▯ —756 baby blue

☐ —355 blue jewel

◉ —507 forest green

⊡ —011 white

◪ —640 blue-violet

⊙ —466 tan

☒ —510 olive

◭ —132 fawn beige

■ —180 dark gray

Tassels: (Make two.) Leave label on one skein of forest green tapestry yarn. From another skein, cut a 6-inch length of forest green. Slip this strand under the folds of yarn to one end of skein. Tie a knot in this strand. Cut another strand of yarn, about 12 inches in length. Wrap this strand tightly around the skein of yarn—about ½ inch to 1 inch below previously tied strand. Tie this strand securely. Cut through all loops at other end of skein and remove label.

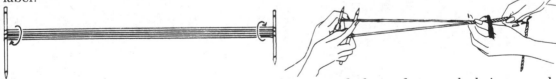

Cord: Use two skeins of forest green yarn. Tie one end of yarn from each skein around a pencil. Loop yarn over a second pencil held about 72 inches from first (you will need a second person to help you with this). Then loop yarn over first pencil and back to second pencil (see illustration). Continue in this manner, using all yarn from the two skeins. Now each person twists pencil with one twisting clockwise and the other twisting counterclockwise, keeping yarn taut. When yarn begins to kink, let one person hold center of yarn while other person holds both pencils. Gradually release yarn, letting it twist.

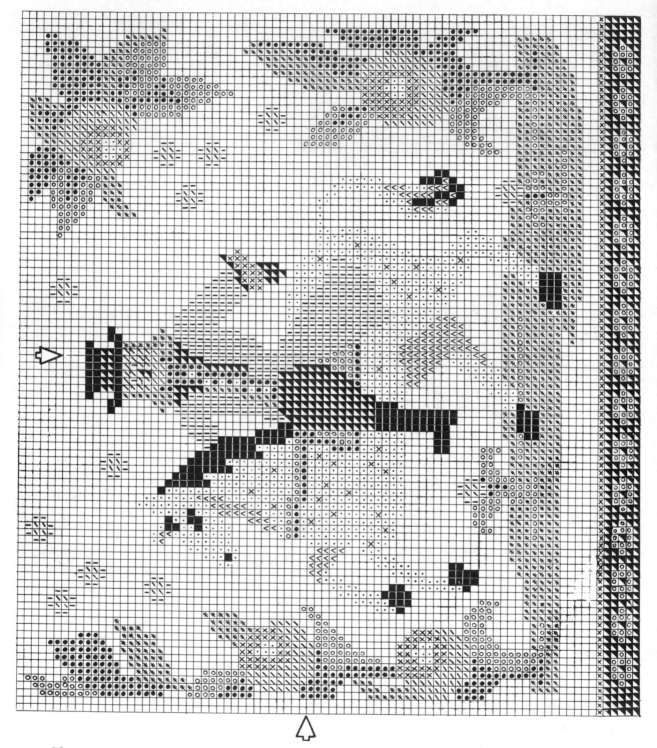

THREE GEOMETRIC PILLOWS

These pillows are all done in geometric patterns with knitting worsted.

The beauty of needlepoint lies in its texture—the evenness of the stitches. The yarn should not be pulled tight—it will stretch and become uneven when it is pulled. Just let the yarn relax between the meshes and, when pulling yarn to front, pull a few inches at a time, not a long stretch of yarn in one motion.

When you start a design, it is important that the first section be absolutely correct, since this is your guide for the rest of the design. Go very slowly, following graphs and diagrams, and counting meshes carefully.

TRIANGLE TWIRL PILLOW (approximate finished size 13-by-13 inches)

MATERIALS

Mono canvas #12 (12 single meshes per inch) 17-by-17 inches

Coats & Clark's "Red Heart" Knitting Worsted, 4-Ply ("tangle-proof" pull-out skeins), about ½-ounce each of:

    No. 253 tangerine
    No. 255 burnt orange
    No. 848 skipper blue
    No. 850 cobalt blue
    No. 511 staccato blue
    No. 514 deep turquoise

Coats & Clark's #18 tapestry needle

½-yard deep blue wool fabric or velveteen, for back of pillow (or one piece, about 15-by-15 inches)

½-yard muslin for inner pillow

J. & P. Coats Super Sheen® Mercerized Sewing or dual duty plus thread to match back of pillow

Polyester batting; masking tape

Securing Ends of Yarn: When starting, leave a 2-inch end at back of canvas. While working on right side, manipulate this end with your fingers so that it will be caught in back of the first few stitches.

When ending, put needle to back of canvas; thread through back of last few stitches and cut.

Needlework: This design is made up of rows of interlocking triangles, all exactly the same size. All stitches are straight and perpendicular to the outer edges of the pillow. Use a single strand of yarn and do not pull yarn tight.

Bind all edges of canvas with masking tape to prevent raveling. Mark TOP of canvas.

Triangle Stitch: Mark a square in center of canvas, 18 meshes on all sides. Draw diagonal lines from corner to corner, making four triangles, as shown (1).

Starting in center square of canvas and following diagram for color, work triangles 1 through 4; turn canvas for each triangle (2).

Note: Center stitch of each triangle starts in same (center) hole.

Now that the center of the design has been established, it is not necessary to mark the rest of the design.

Color Key

= skipper blue OR coral
= cobalt blue OR burnt orange
= staccato blue OR light coral
= deep turquoise OR coral shell
= burnt orange OR peach
= tangerine OR off white

Alternate Yarn Choice:

Red Heart Persian-Type Yarn (12-yard skeins):

#005—off white		3
#988—peach		3
#436—coral shell		3
#852—light coral		2
#843—coral		1
#958—burnt orange		1

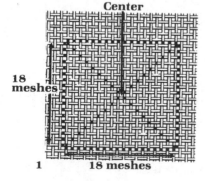

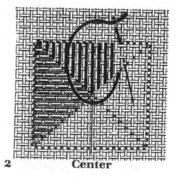

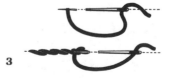

Following numbers and colors on diagram, work in rows of interlocking triangles around center square (note on diagram where corners are formed). Make one complete row around center square before beginning another. Continue, following graph to complete pattern.

Note: In each succeeding row, long edges of triangles are back-to-back with previous row.

When pattern has been completed, finish the edge with a border in deep blue to match backing. Work straight stitches over three meshes; form a miter at each corner by working over one mesh less with each stitch. To emphasize pattern, separate orange sections from blue sections by outlining with stem stitches in deep blue to match border. Work stem from left to right over about six meshes, as shown (3).

To complete pillow, see **Finishing.**

INDIAN PILLOW (approximate finished size 17-by-17 inches)

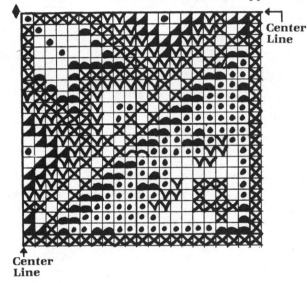

Center Line

Center Line

Color Key

⊡ = cardinal

⊠ = skipper blue

⊠ = light olive

◪ = yellow

☐ = white

◒ = turquoise

MATERIALS

Mono canvas #10 (10 single meshes per inch) 19-by-19 inches

Coats & Clark's "Red Heart" Knitting Worsted, 4-Ply ("tangle-proof" pull-out skeins), about 1 ounce each of:

No. 919 cardinal
No. 1 white
No. 848 skipper blue
No. 651 light olive
No. 227 canary yellow
No. 515 dark turquoise

Coats & Clark's #18 tapestry needle

½-yard wool fabric or velveteen in one of the colors used, for back of pillow (or one piece, about 18-by-18 inches)

17-square-inch knife-edge pillow

J. & P. Coats Super Sheen® Mercerized Sewing or dual duty plus thread to match back of pillow

Masking tape

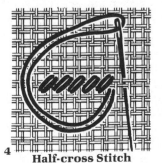

4   **Half-cross Stitch**

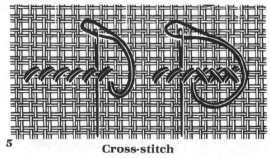

5   **Cross-stitch**

Needlework: Bind all edges of canvas with masking tape to prevent raveling. One inch is allowed for seams. Mark center across both ways with a line of basting stitches. Crossing of basting stitches is ♦ on chart. The chart shows one-fourth of the entire design. Design is worked in blocks of four straight stitches worked over four threads. Each square of chart represents one block. Use single strand of yarn throughout. Starting at center where basting stitches cross and ♦ on chart, follow chart and Color Key for design. Work remaining three-fourths to correspond.

Inner Pillow: Cut two pieces of muslin ½ inch larger than finished edges of needlework. Stitch them together in a ½-inch seam leaving an opening. Turn and stuff compactly; slipstitch opening closed.

Pillow Backing: Pin right side of backing and canvas together. Using zipper foot attachment, machine-stitch very close to outer row of needlepoint, leaving a 10-inch opening in center of one side to insert inner pillow. Stitch around twice. Trim corners diagonally and trim seam allowance; turn to right side. Place inner pillow in needlepoint pillow. Slipstitch opening closed.

To complete pillow, see **Finishing.**

RAINBOW PILLOW (approximate finished size 14-by-14 inches)

MATERIALS

Penelope canvas #5 (five double meshes per inch) 18-by-18 inches

Coats & Clark's Craft & Rug Yarn (140-yard skeins)
  #001 white   two skeins
  #848 skipper blue   one skein

10 yards each of following:
  #261 maize
  #243 orange
  #253 tangerine
  #900 melon
  #588 amethyst
  #814 robin blue

#515 dark turquoise
#676 emerald

#14 or $15 tapestry needle
½-yard wool fabric or velveteen in one of the colors used, for back of pillow (or one piece, about 16-by-16 inches)
14-square-inch knife-edge pillow form
J. & P. Coats Super Sheen® Mercerized Sewing or dual duty plus thread to match back of pillow
Masking tape

Needlework: Bind all edges of canvas with masking tape to prevent raveling. Mark top of canvas. At lower left corner, measure 2 inches in from edge on two adjacent sides; mark to form right angle. Working from diamond on corner, follow graph to make design.

All stitches are worked with a double strand of yarn in half-cross stitch except for those marked with an X, which are worked in cross-stitch in skipper blue.

Note: Each square on graph equals one double mesh on canvas. The graph is keyed with color symbols, so as you work, simply count squares to find number of stitches to be worked in each color.

Half-cross Stitch: This stitch is worked diagonally over one double thread of penelope canvas, with all stitches going in the same direction—from lower left to upper right. Unless you work in long rows, always work with the top of canvas away from you, do not turn it around. Do not pull yarn tight.

Always bring needle to front of canvas at bottom of stitch to be made. When working from left to right (4), insert needle one mesh above and one mesh to side; bring it out again at bottom of next stitch, as shown.

Work each area of the design in the appropriate color.

Cross-stitch: Stitches are marked with an X. Begin by forming half-cross stitches. Complete cross-stitch by working back across the half-cross stitches (5).

Finishing: When design is complete, check to see if it has lost its shape. If there is no distortion, steam-press on wrong side, using a damp press cloth. If needlepoint is distorted, it will have to be blocked: Place canvas right-side-down on a well-padded board. Using extra heavy pins, pin canvas to board (at unworked edges), keeping pins close and stretching canvas to correct shape as you pin. If needlepoint is slightly distorted, steam-press with a wet press cloth and let dry. If needlepoint is greatly distorted, wet canvas back thoroughly and leave pinned to board until completely dry.

Machine-stitch around finished edge about four times to keep seam allowance from raveling. Trim canvas 1 inch away from edge of needlework.

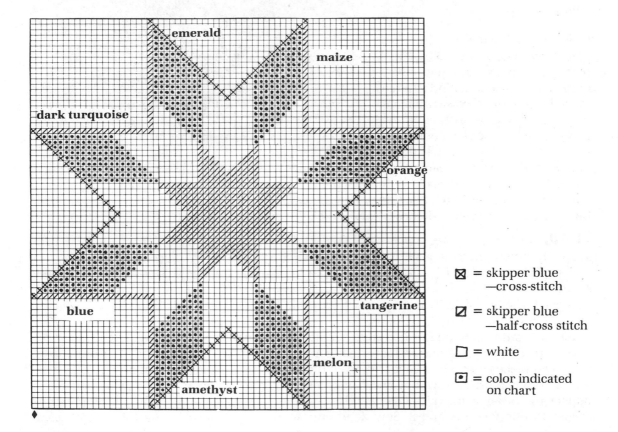

☒ = skipper blue
—cross-stitch

◿ = skipper blue
—half-cross stitch

☐ = white

⊡ = color indicated
on chart

FARMER TOY

(Toy measures 5-by-11½ inches.)

MATERIALS

Coats & Clark's Red Heart® "Wintuk," 4-ply, Art E. 267 (4 ounce ready-to-use pull-out skeins): 3 yards of No. 737 pink; 6 yards of No. 230 yellow; 8 yards of No. 814 robin blue; 15 yards each of No. 245 orange and No. 902 jockey red; 20 yards each of No. 1 white and No. 737 pink; 50 yards each of No. 12 black and No. 818 blue jewel

14-by-19-inch piece of single-thread canvas, 10 meshes per inch

J. & P. Coats #18 tapestry needle

Scraps of pink felt for ears; a 4-by-6-inch piece of gold felt for brim; a 6-by-12-inch piece of blue felt for gusset

Stuffing

From canvas, cut two 7-by-9-inch pieces for body; two 5-by-5-inch pieces for arms; and two 6-by-7-inch pieces for head. Bind all edges of each piece of canvas with masking tape to prevent raveling. Designs are worked in continental stitch. Each stitch is worked over one thread of canvas; each square on charts represents one thread of canvas. Leaving about 1-inch margin all around, follow charts and Color and Stitch Key. Make one Chart 1 and one Chart 2 for body; two Chart 3 for arms; and one Chart 4 and one Chart 5 for head. Embroider the straight stitches where indicated on charts.

Finishing: To block, steam-press embroidered pieces on right side, stretching to correct shape. If steam-pressing is not sufficient, block as follows: Place piece right side up on a well-padded board, using rustproof pins, pin to board along edges, stretching to correct shape as you pin. Wet piece thoroughly and leave pinned to board until completely dry. Remove from board. With orange, work loop stitches (see stitch details) on head, covering all orange stitches. Do not cut loops.

   Machine-stitch around finished edge of embroidery to prevent raveling. Turn raw edges of each piece to wrong side and sew neatly in place. With wrong sides together and black, sew head pieces together all around, inserting some stuffing. Fold one arm section in half and with wrong sides together and black, inserting stuffing, sew along three open sides. Repeat for other arm. With wrong sides together and black, sew body pieces together across top between A and B. Sew head and arms to body. From blue felt, cut gussets, following diagrams. Place side gussets along sides of body and sew in place. Insert stuffing and sew bottom gusset in place. Cut two ears from pink felt and sew to sides of head; cut brim from gold felt and slip over top of head. Sew in place along black line above hair.

Color and Stitch Key

Continental Stitch

⊡ = white
⊠ = black
⊙ = robin blue
☐ = blue jewel
▣ = pink
⊞ = light pink
⊟ = yellow
◪ = orange
◣ = jockey red

Straight stitch
— = black

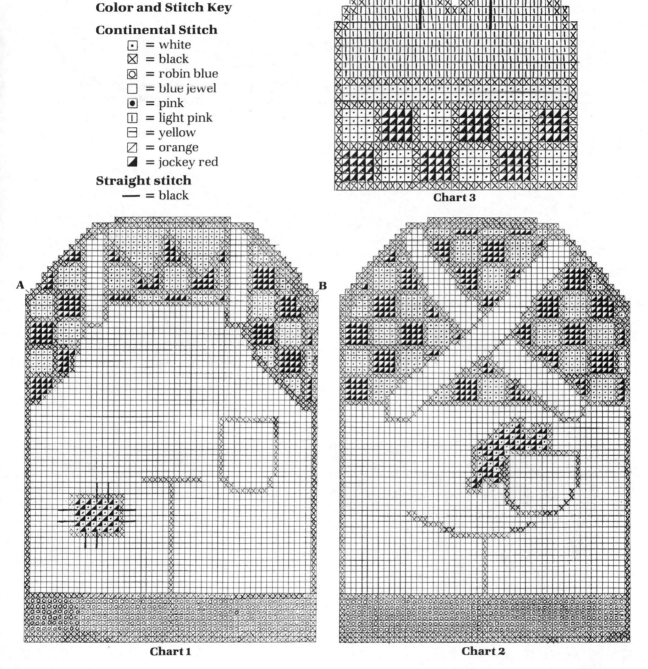

Chart 3

Chart 1

Chart 2

Loop Stitch: Insert needle from right to left under a thread, bring needle out to front of work (see Fig. 1), with left thumb hold down ½-inch of free end, with yarn above the stitch; insert needle from right to left under next thread (Fig. 2) and pull up tightly to complete loop stitch. Holding yarn down with left thumb to make a ½-inch loop, insert needle from right to left under next thread (Fig. 3). Then using next thread complete loop stitch as before.

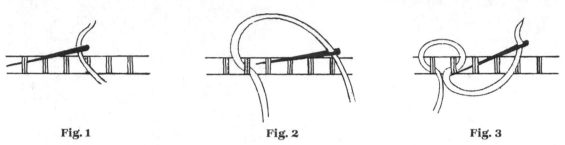

Fig. 1   Fig. 2   Fig. 3

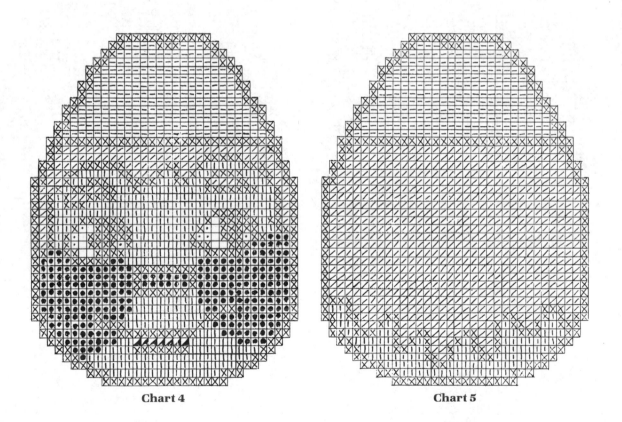

Chart 4   Chart 5

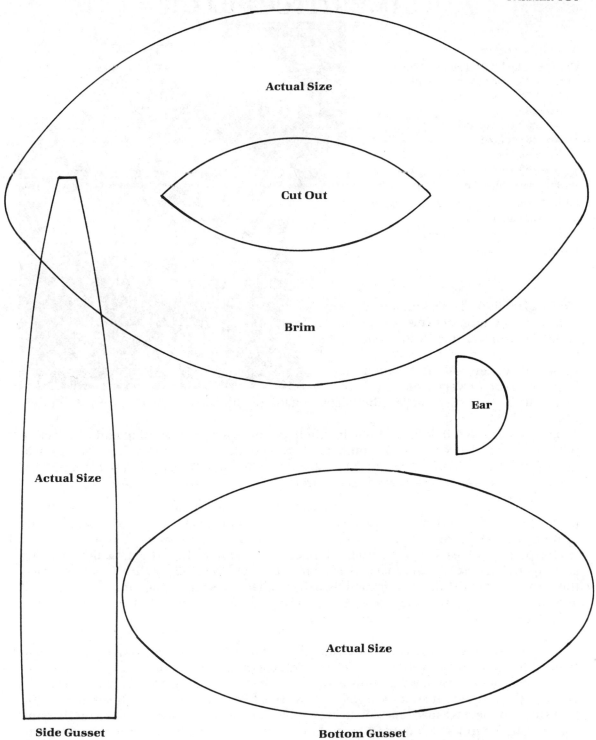

Actual Size

Cut Out

Brim

Ear

Actual Size

Side Gusset

Bottom Gusset

Actual Size

FLAME STITCH PILLOW

MATERIALS

Coats & Clark's Red Heart 4-Ply Hand-
knitting Yarn: 1 ounce each of:
- No. 251 vibrant orange
- No. 255 burnt orange
- No. 253 tangerine
- No. 261 maize
- No. 586 lilac
- No. 588 amethyst

#18 tapestry needle

One 17-inch square of 12-mesh canvas
(single-thread canvas)

One 13-inch-square pillow and ½-yard
wool or velveteen for back of pillow

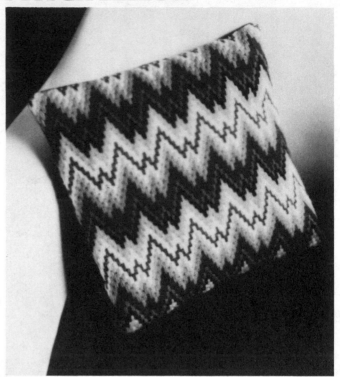

To Begin: Bind all edges of canvas
with masking tape to prevent raveling. Measure 2 inches in from
the two adjacent sides of lower
left-hand corner and mark with a
basting thread or very light pencil
marks to form a right angle. The edges outside of the corner markings are to be left
unworked.

Design is worked in straight Gobelin stitch (see diagram) in ascending and descending
pattern, worked over varying numbers of canvas threads. (The canvas threads will
hereafter be described as "meshes.") The straight Gobelin stitch is simply a straight vertical
stitch worked over several threads at one time.

Stitching: Use a single strand of yarn throughout, taking care not to let the strand
become twisted. If it does so, hold the canvas up and let the yarn and needle dangle, thus
"untwisting" the yarn.

The pattern of each row consists of six tall flames and five short flames. See the
accompanying diagram and chart. Be sure to count very carefully on the first row across
the canvas. After the first row is established, all other rows follow the same pattern of tall
and short flames so that such close attention will not be necessary. Notice, however, that
the mesh count does vary from row to row.

First Row: Starting at A on chart, with amethyst and leaving a 5-inch end, bring needle to
front at the right angle you marked at lower left corner, insert needle five meshes directly
above, bring it out five meshes below and one mesh to the right (see Fig. 1). Note that when
you are working over five meshes, you are covering five threads and four holes. Repeat the
first stitch in the next space at right, bring needle out one mesh below and one mesh to the
right as shown in Fig. 2. Continue to point of flame, following the diagram. To return to

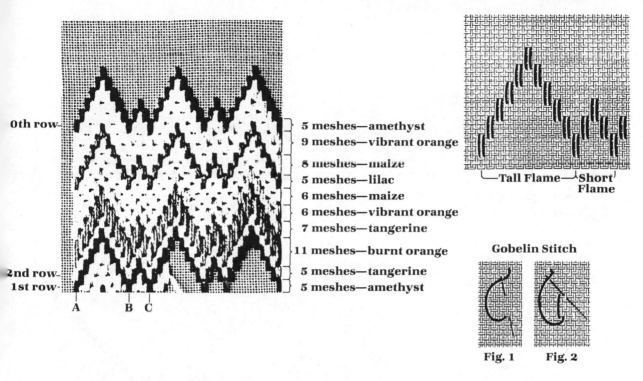

0th row

2nd row
1st row

A   B C

5 meshes—amethyst
9 meshes—vibrant orange

8 meshes—maize
5 meshes—lilac
6 meshes—maize
6 meshes—vibrant orange
7 meshes—tangerine

11 meshes—burnt orange

5 meshes—tangerine
5 meshes—amethyst

Tall Flame Short
Flame

Gobelin Stitch

Fig. 1   Fig. 2

lower edge, bring needle out nine meshes below and one mesh to the right. Continue downward, working stitches over five meshes as before.

Working in this manner, follow chart from A to C five times, then from A to B once to complete first row. Bring needle to back of canvas and draw through last few stitches to fasten yarn. When working Gobelin stitches, it is wise to first run the needle through several stitches in one direction and then in the opposite direction to secure them. Join new color at beginning of row in same manner.

Using color and number of meshes to be worked over in each succeeding row as indicated, follow chart until tenth row has been completed. Repeat second through tenth row once, then repeat second through fourth rows once more. Fill in free spaces at top, using color and number of meshes as for fifth through eighth rows; fill in spaces at bottom as for seventh, eighth, and ninth rows.

Steam-press piece on wrong side, stretching to correct shape. Use a damp pressing cloth and do not let iron rest on piece. Use a very light touch! If piece is badly out of shape, block as follows: Place canvas right side down on a well-padded board. Using rustproof pins, pin to board along edges, stretching to correct shape as you pin. Wet canvas thoroughly and leave pinned to board until completely dry.

Machine-stitch around edge of needlework about four times to keep seam allowance from raveling after it is trimmed. For pillow back, cut fabric 2 inches larger than finished needlework (1 inch allowed all around for seams). With right sides together, sew back to canvas along three sides. Insert pillow and sew remaining edges together, turning under seam allowances.

STRAWBERRY CLOCK

MATERIALS

One 16-inch square of 14-count ivory
Aida fabric for cross-stitch

OR

One 18-inch square of 12-mesh mono
canvas for needlepoint
One 14-inch octagonal frame
Battery-operated clock mechanism
and clock hands

For Needlepoint Version Only:
one 40-yard skein of sea foam #227
or desired color for the background

	COLOR	BRUNSANA PERSIAN YARN	NO. OF 32-INCH STRANDS	DMC FLOSS (1 skein each)
Δ	dark red	82	[8]	321
x	medium red	103	[8]	666
⊓	pale pink	174	[2]	818
–	white	34	[15]	snow
o	medium yellow	230	[4]	744
▲	medium gold	184	[4]	725
♦	dark brown	65	[4]	801
X	medium brown	67	[4]	433
♦	black	35	[4]	310
⌗	light blue	68	[4]	800
*	medium blue	56	[4]	799
●	dark blue	107	[4]	797
◆	light green	201	[15]	472
	medium-light green	200	[8]	471
■	medium-dark green	19	[8]	469
	dark green	18	[8]	937

84

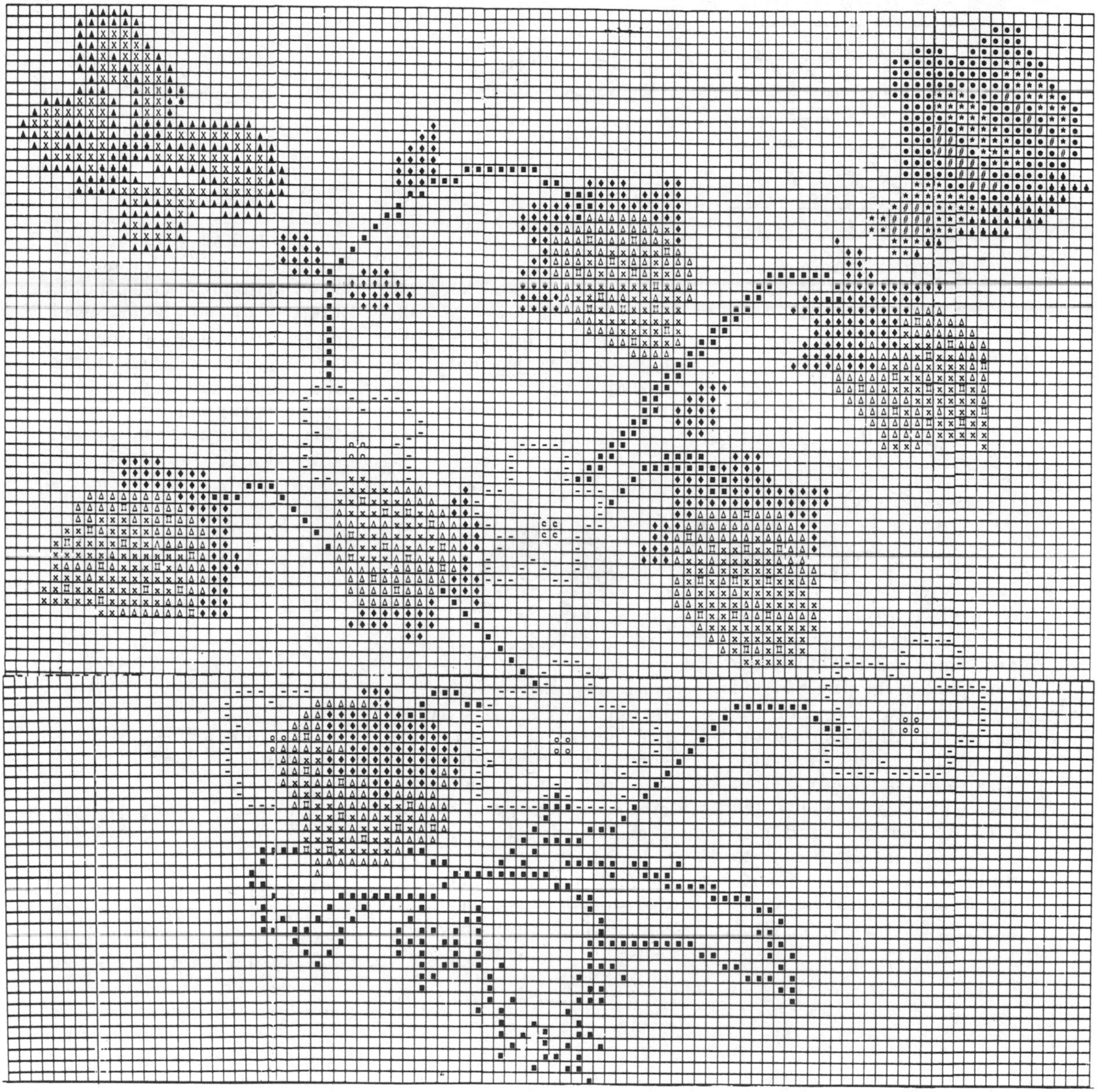

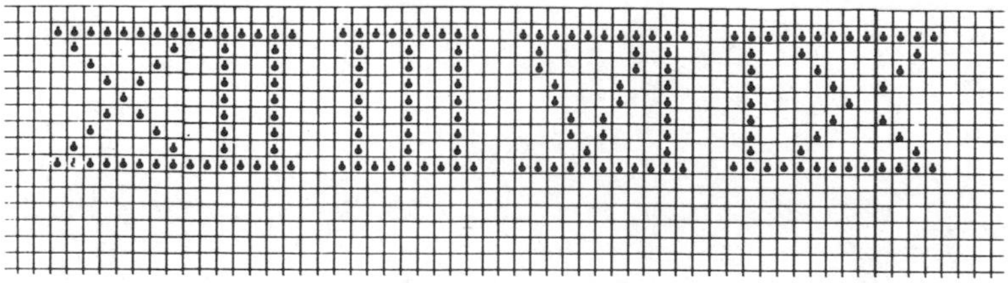

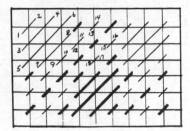

Chequer Stitch

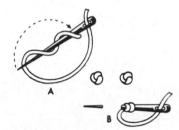

French Knots: Bring the thread out at the required position. Hold the thread down with the left thumb and wind the thread twice around the needle (A). Still holding the thread firmly, twist the needle back to the starting point and insert it close to where the thread first emerged (see arrow). Pull thread through to the back and secure for a single French knot or pass on to the position of the next stitch (B).

Chain Stitch: Bring the thread out at top of line and hold down with left thumb. Insert the needle where it last emerged and bring the point out a short distance away. Pull the thread through, keeping the working thread under the needle point.

Long and Short Stitch: This form of satin stitch is so named as all the stitches are of varying lengths. It is often used to fill a shape that is too large or too irregular to be covered by satin stitch. It is also used to achieve a shaded effect, as shown. In the first row the stitches are alternately long and short and closely follow the outline of the shape. In the following rows long and short stitches are worked to give a smooth texture.

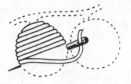

Satin Stitch: Work straight stitch across the shape as shown. If desired, chain stitch or running stitch may be worked first to form a padding underneath, to give a raised effect. Care must be taken to keep a good edge. Do not make the stitches too long, as then they could be pulled out of position. Satin stitch can also be worked over counted threads of even-weave fabric. In this case, the stitches are taken over the desired number of threads and are worked one stitch between each two adjacent threads of the fabric.

Straight Stitch: (also known as Single Satin Stitch) This is shown as single, spaced stitches worked either in a regular or irregular manner. Sometimes the stitches are of varying size. The stitches should be neither too long nor too loose.

Preparing Materials: Machine-stitch a narrow hem around all edges of the Aida cloth to prevent raveling OR for the needlepoint version, tape all edges of the canvas with masking tape for the same purpose.

Find the center of the fabric or canvas by first folding it in half lengthwise. Mark the fold line with a basting thread. Then fold in half in other direction and again mark with basting thread. The point where the threads cross will be the center of your fabric or canvas. Apply a thin layer of all-purpose glue covering a four-stitch square. When all work is completed, this area will be snipped out in order to insert the clock mechanism. No stitches are worked in that square.

Notes: Each full strand of Persian yarn can easily be divided into three separate strands and each full strand of embroidery floss consists of six separate strands. When you are instructed to use one, two, or three strands, this means that you are to use that many of the separate strands, not that number of full strands.

The strawberries, butterflies, clock numerals, and small leaves are to be worked in continental stitch for the needlepoint and in cross-stitch on the Aida fabric, using two strands of yarn or floss in the needle. It is suggested that you work the following crewel embroidery stitches for the remaining design elements: Work the blossom petals in satin stitch and the blossom centers in French knots. The large leaves at the bottom of the design are first outlined using dark green and a back stitch. Fill in the leaves with long and short stitch, using one strand each of medium-dark green and medium-light green in the same needle. For the top part of the leaves (see photograph), use single strands of light- and medium-light green in the same needle. Work stems in chain stitch with one strand of dark green. This method of stitching is optional. Entire design may be worked in continental or cross-stitch, if preferred.

Border: After the design area is completed, lay your frame over the piece, centering it carefully. Then, mark with basting threads the area you need to cover for your border. In this area, work the chequer stitch for the needlepoint version. In this stitch, your needle is brought up in the odd-numbered squares and down through the even-numbered squares. The heavier lines are worked in green and the thinner lines are worked in white. For the cross-stitch version, work one green cross-stitch at each point where a bold line crosses a graph line. If you wish, you may also make white cross-stitches where the thin lines cross the graph lines.

MONOGRAMMED PLAID TOTE

MATERIALS

7-mesh plastic canvas—three sheets approximately 10½-by-13 inches

Acrylic yarn (4-ply, knitting worsted type)—3½ ounces each of Colors A, B, and C and 1 ounce of Color D

#14 or #16 tapestry needle

½-yard lining fabric, if desired

Preparing Canvas: From one sheet of canvas, cut a piece having 78 holes across and 64 rows from top to bottom for front of tote. From second sheet of canvas, cut another piece the same size for back of tote. From third sheet of canvas, cut one piece 78 holes by 13 holes for bottom of tote; two pieces 64 holes by 13 holes for sides of tote; and two pieces three holes by 78 holes for handles.

The handles should be worked first as they will be secured to the tote by working tent stitches through two thicknesses at once. That is, you will hold one end of the handle behind front of purse and stitch through front and handle sections at the same time. Leaving three or four holes unworked at each end work handles in mosaic stitch (see Stitch #4 in Pattern Stitch Section, p. 32).

SUGGESTED COLOR COMBINATIONS

	brown/rust plaid	blue/green plaid	red/black plaid
COLOR A	off white or ecru	white	white
COLOR B	brown	royal or medium blue	black
COLOR C	rust	emerald green	scarlet
COLOR D	light gold	light gold	light gold

Charting Your Monogram: Select the three initials of your monogram from chart. Use the blank space at bottom of alphabet chart to draw in the three initials of your chart. Do this in pencil so that you can experiment with the best spacing. All letters are 16 stitches high but they will vary in width so you must decide on the best spacing for the letters of your choice. Your initials will be larger than they appear on the chart as the chart is 10 to the inch, while your canvas is six to the inch.

Each square of the graph chart equals one stitch. You will have space for 77 stitches across, so use 77 squares on the graph in charting your monogram.

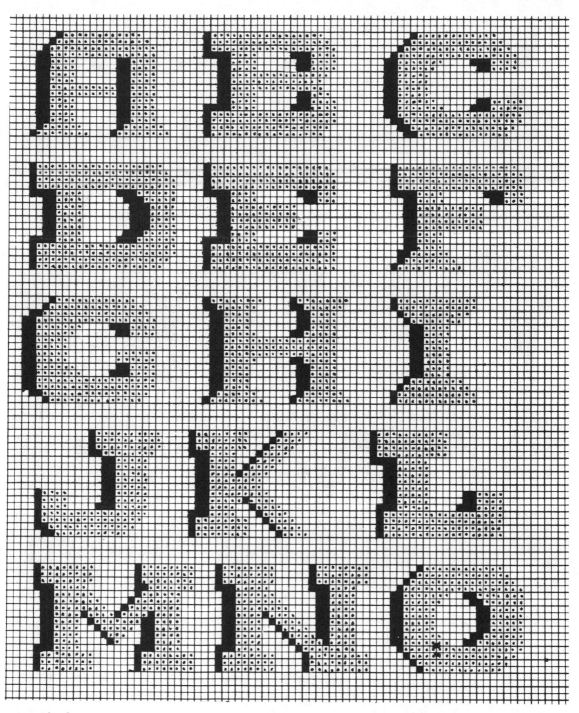

10 per inch

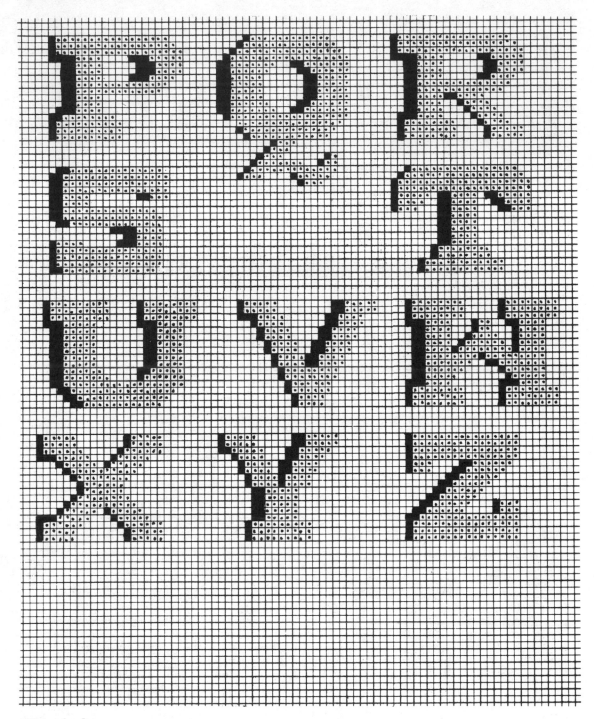

10 per inch

Use two strands of yarn in the needle at all times, taking care to keep them untwisted.

On one of the plastic sheets planned for front or back of tote, work the initials, using Color C (this is designated by a black dot on the chart). Then, do the shading of each initial with Color B (designated by solid black squares on the chart).

Next, overcast the top edge of this piece with Color C. To do this, bring the needle up in the hole in the top right-hand corner. Pass the needle to the back and bring it up in the next hole to the left, thus covering the top edge. Continue across in this manner.

Next, attach handle to purse front. With white sewing thread, baste the ends of the handle in place, having the unworked holes on the wrong side of the front section. Now, work two rows of continental stitch across the top edge (using Color A). As you come to the place where the handles are basted, work through both thicknesses, thus securing the handle to the purse front.

Fill in the balance of the background for monogram panel in continental stitch, using Color A. Then, work two rows of continental stitch, using Color C.

Special Notes on Working Chottie's Plaid: This stitch is very easy to work with just a little practice. There are a few things that are a bit different from the usual needlepoint stitches, however. Be sure to read the following instructions before starting.

1. Slant of stitches. You will notice on the diagram that the stitches slant in a different direction than those worked in continental stitch. For this reason, you must turn your work so that the plaid stitches will match the others on your work. The top is to your right and what would normally be the left side edge is now at the top (see Diagrams).

2. The plaid is worked in two stages. You work all of the horizontal rows first (Diagrams

Diagrams for Chottie's Plaid

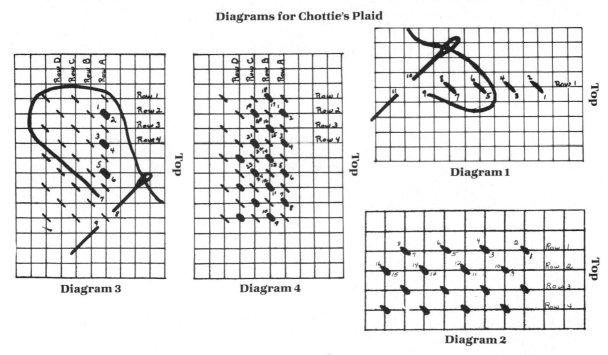

Diagram 3

Diagram 4

Diagram 1

Diagram 2

1 and 2). Notice that you are to work in every other hole, leaving a space between each stitch. If you are working correctly, your stitches will lay in diagonal rows (see Diagram 2). After all of the horizontal rows are worked, you work the vertical rows, filling in the skipped stitches while holding the canvas in the same position. In Diagrams 3 and 4, the stitches of the vertical rows are shown as heavier lines or markings.

3. Also notice that on Row 2 and all even-numbered rows you start one stitch in from the first stitch of Row 1 and work one stitch beyond the last stitch of the first row.

4. Color progression: This means the sequence of colors, row by row. The plaid as shown is a four-color plaid. If you wish to practice the plaid on a scrap piece of canvas, you can try it with just two colors (this will make a houndstooth check). For practice, work two rows with Color A, then two with Color C. Continue to alternate in this way until you have about eight rows. Now, work the vertical rows, following the same color sequence. When you have finished your two-color practice piece, you are now ready to start the plain portion of your purse.

With the top of the purse front section held to the right and with two strands of Color A in your needle, work Row 1 of Diagram 1 along the edge that is now the top of your work. Each of the two strands of yarn in your needle should be approximately 26 inches long. This can vary with each individual so experiment to find the correct length you will need to complete one row.

Continue to work the horizontal rows as shown in Diagrams 1 and 2, following the color progression shown below. (You have already worked one row, so on this first color progression, work just three more rows of Color A for a total of four rows of this color.)

COLOR PROGRESSION:
Work four rows— Color A
Work one row—   Color D
Work three rows—Color B
Work one row—   Color D
Work three rows—Color B
Work four rows— Color C
Work two rows—   Color A
Work one row—   Color D

When front of purse is completed, work another identical piece for back of purse. For side sections, work each piece, starting at top edge, with 20 rows of continental stitch in Color A, two rows of continental in Color C, with balance of piece worked in plaid, following color progression above. For the botton of purse, work in Color B, using continental, mosaic, or any stitch of your choice.

To Join Sections: Hold two sections together with wrong sides facing each other and "lace" them together using same overcast stitch as used on top of each of the other pieces and on side edges of handles. Line, if desired.

SPRING BASKETS

MATERIALS

Darice pastel plastic 10-mesh canvas—four sheets of the same color will make all three items or if you make each in a different color you will need two sheets for each basket and one sheet for the "flower box"

#18 or #20 tapestry needle

Tapestry yarn, Persian-type needlepoint yarn, light-weight knitting worsted-type yarns (or any yarn that will pass easily through the canvas while still giving good coverage) in amounts given for each project (all yardages are approximate)

The yarn recommended for trim, borders, and joining is a deeper shade of the same color as the Darice canvas used for that item

No background stitches are required—simply let the colored canvas show

The lines of each chart represent the ribs or threads of the canvas. The blank squares represent the holes of the canvas. Each symbol denotes one stitch to be made with the color represented by that symbol (see the four stitch charts).

Handles: Work one of the finishing stitches along each long edge of the handle. Attach one short end of the handle in center of top edge of one side of basket so that three rows of holes of handle extend below the top edge of the side, basting it in place if desired. Next, work the border design of your choice across the top edge, working through both thicknesses when you reach the handle, thus attaching the handle neatly and securely. Attach the other end of the handle to opposite side in the same manner. Next, complete all other border stitches on all four pieces. (No stitches are worked on the bottom piece.)

Border Stitches: On the Easter basket, an alternating color mosaic stitch was used. One mosaic stitch was worked in a medium shade with the next one in a light shade, alternating the two colors throughout the border.

A solid color mosaic stitch was used for the flower box.

The slanting Gobelin stitch was used for the tulip basket.

Joining and Finishing: Join each of the four sides of the baskets or box to the bottom piece using the overcasting (also called whipping or lacing stitch). Then using the same stitch or Terry's picot edging, join each side piece to the adjoining side piece. You will find it easier to work from bottom to top.

Then finish the top edges using either the overcast stitch or Terry's picot edging. If a single strand of yarn does not cover the edges adequately, use a double strand.

FLOWER BOX

Color code and yardages sufficient for front and backs worked with a three-flower motif and two sides worked with a single flower motif.

Flower—color of your choice (10 yards)

Leaves—bright green (8 yards)

Trim—deeper shade, same color as the canvas (15 yards)

Cut one piece for back and one piece for front each with 57 holes across and 41 holes down. Cut two pieces each with 31 holes across and 41 holes down for sides. Cut one piece with 57 holes across and 31 holes down for the bottom.

Work design areas first on the front, backs, and sides, then see stitch charts for borders and general direction for joining and finishing.

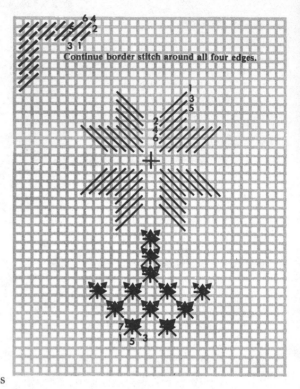

Continue border stitch around all four edges.

Flower Box Sides

/ Flower color

Smyrna stitch
Bright green for leaves

Flower Box Front & Back

/ Tent stitch
Flower color

✕ Cross-stitch
Same color as flower

Smyrna stitch
Same color as flower

↗ Tent stitch
Bright green for leaves

✕ Cross-stitch
Same color as leaves

Continue border stitch around all four edges.

94

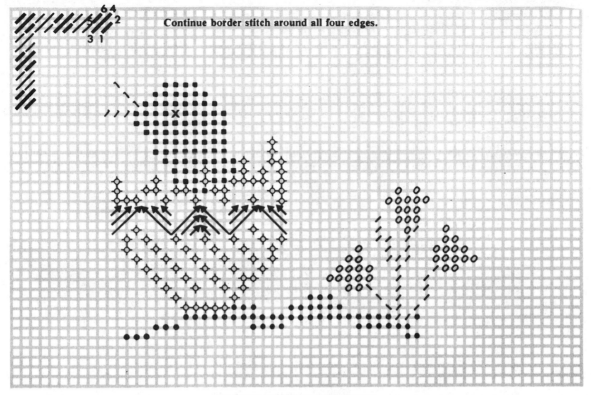

Continue border stitch around all four edges.

BABY CHICK BASKET

Color codes and yardages are sufficient for four sides worked alike.

Baby chick—yellow or gold (4 yards)

Eye—blue (1 yard)

Beak—orange (1 yard)

Easter egg—bright color of your choice (6 yards)

Easter egg trim—(4 yards)

Flower—color of your choice (4 yards)

Leaves—light green (4 yards)

Trim—deeper shade, same color as the canvas (20 yards)

Cut four pieces each with 59 holes across and 39 holes down for sides. Cut one piece with 59 holes in each direction for bottom. Cut one piece 12 holes wide and 11 inches in length for handle.

First, work design on each of four side pieces, following the chart for design placement. Before working top borders, see general directions for attaching handles and see stitch chart for border. Also see general directions for joining and finishing tips.

Baby Chick Basket

- ■ Yellow or gold for baby chick
- ✗ Blue for eye (cross-stitch)
- ↖ Orange for beak
- ◇ Bright color of your choice for Easter egg
- ↑ Easter egg trim color of your choice
- O Flower in color of your choice
- ╱ Light green for leaves
- ● Dark green

Except for the borders and Easter egg trim, the designs are worked in a tent stitch.

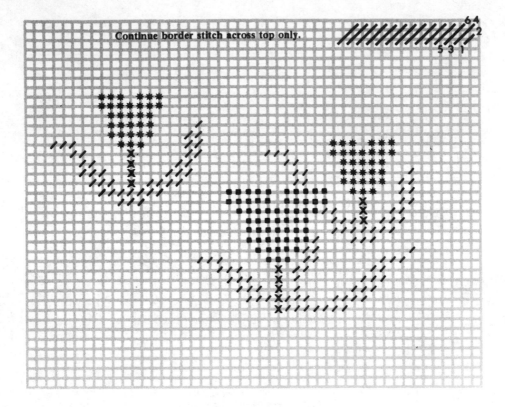

TULIP BASKET

Color codes and yardages are sufficient for working all four sides alike.

Center tulip—medium shade, color of your choice (5 yards)

Two smaller tulips—darker shade, color of your choice (8 yards)

Leaves—bright green (8 yards)

Trim—deeper shade, same color as the canvas (18 yards)

Cut four pieces each with 47 holes across and 38 holes down for the four side pieces. Cut one piece with 47 holes in each direction for bottom. Cut one piece with 10 holes across and 11 inches in length for handle.

Working order: First work tulip design on each of two sides placing them as shown on the chart or in any way that seems pleasing to you. Before working top borders, see general directions for attaching handles and see stitch chart for border. Also see general directions for joining and finishing tips.

Tulip Basket

- ■ Center tulip—medium shade of color of your choice
- ✳ Two smaller tulips—darker shade of color of your choice
- ∕ Bright green for leaves
- ✗ Cross-stitch—same color as leaves

Except for the border and cross-stitch, the designs are worked in a tent stitch.

TULIP-TIME BOXES

MATERIALS

7-mesh pastel plastic canvas: three sheets are required to make a box 6¼-by-6½-by-5¼ inches (smaller boxes can be made from one or two sheets or even from scraps of canvas)

Yarn choices: Persian-type needle-point yarn; tapestry yarn; 4-ply knitting worsted. You will need approximately 8 yards green for the leaves and 40 yards for flowers and borders.

#16 or #18 tapestry needle

Cutting the Canvas: For front and back of box, cut two pieces, each having 43 holes across and 35 holes down. For sides of box, cut two pieces, each having 40 holes across and 35 holes down. For top and bottom of box, cut two pieces, each having 40 holes across and 43 holes down.

Borders: Work a border of three-stitch Scotch stitch around all edges of top piece. Leaving back edge unworked, overcast three remaining edges. Work same type of border on top and bottom edges only of each of the four side pieces. (Do not overcast edges on any of these pieces at this time.)

Designs: Following one of the charts given, work designs on each side piece and on top of box.

With colored canvas, it is not necessary to fill in background. Take care, however, not to run yarn from one design motif to another across empty squares. When you complete one motif, secure the yarn and start over for the next design.

The tulip-time box borders are to be worked in Scotch stitch, which is a "three-thread" pattern. To work this type of pattern, you need to have a number of holes evenly divisible by three plus one additional hole. The cutting directions previously given have allowed for this. If another pattern stitch appeals to you more, you might need to adjust the size of one or more pieces. To work any of the following "two-thread" stitches, you should have an uneven number of holes: rice stitch, mosaic stitch, Smyrna stitch.

The flower motifs are to be worked in continental or half-cross stitch. While either is satisfactory for this type of project, I would suggest that you select the continental.

In the Design Chart, all slanting lines are shown exactly as they are worked. For the leaves, the stitch is started at one of the lower black circles and ends at the upper circle. Note that in each leaf, all stitches end in same hole. For the flowers, each symbol represents one stitch. For clarity, the symbols are shown in blank squares. Actually, each stitch is, of course, worked over one mesh. Work the design as shown for top of box. Arrange the tulip motifs in same way for sides of box or, if you prefer, rearrange them in some other way. Notice in the photograph that only the small-size tulip was used on front of box and that they were arranged diagonally. Or, select one of the Alternate Flower Designs. Better yet, make several boxes and use a different design for each.

Tulip stem and leaves: The stems are worked in cross-stitch. The leaves are designed to be worked in long, slanting stitches, but can be worked in continental or half-cross, if desired.

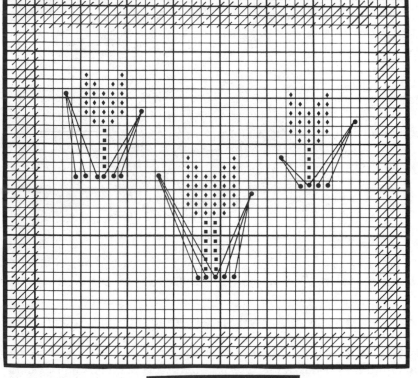

Design Chart

♦ —main color

■ —leaf green

Long, straight lines beside each flower represent the leaves. Work these in green.

Work Scotch stitch border in main color.

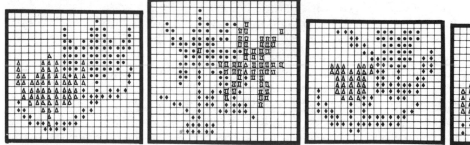

Alternate Flower Designs

Wherever you see the symbol: ♦, you should use green. For all other symbols, use the color of your choice.

LEARN-A-STITCH TOTE I

MATERIALS

Three sheets of 7-mesh plastic canvas in pastel colors of your choice

One skein of yarn—4-ply Wintuk in knitting worsted-weight

#16 or #18 tapestry needle

⅓-yard fabric for lining

Cutting Directions: From one sheet of canvas, cut one piece so that you have 75 holes across and 51 holes down. Cut an identical piece from another sheet of canvas.

From each of these sheets, cut a strap handle five holes wide along one of the long edges of sheet, having the strap at least 91 holes in length.

From third sheet of canvas, cut piece for bottom so that it has 75 holes in length and 17 holes in width. Cut two pieces, each having 51 holes by 17 holes.

With a sharp razor or with scissors, trim all edges so that they are completely smooth.

Start with the strap handle. Leave three rows of empty holes at one end of strap. Then work 42 rows of Smyrna stitch with each row having two Smyrna stitches across. Place second strap piece under first piece and whip the two long edges together along both side edges. Set finished strap aside. Next, work a border of Smyrna stitches around all four edges of front of tote. When you are working the top border, secure strap in the center by placing one of the unworked edges of strap under the front piece at center top. At this point, work through both thicknesses (strap piece and front piece), thus securing strap to front. Next work the design of your choice on front piece. Work the back piece in the same manner. Work border of Smyrna stitches around all four edges of both side pieces.

Following Design Charts: Each symbol on the charts represents one complete Smyrna stitch. As you already know if you have done some practice stitches each stitch covers two threads of canvas in each direction.

I recommend that you start by working the border around all four sides before starting the design.

If you choose to work the design at the top start counting from the upper left corner. Including the corner stitch, count across five stitches. Your first design stitch will fall just under this fifth stitch.

Look at the chart and count across five symbols. In the square just below, you will see a symbol plus the number 1. This is the first design stitch. Now, look in the row below. Start the next design stitch at the point where you see a symbol and the number 2. Then, working from left to right, work four more stitches in that row. Or, if you prefer, you can

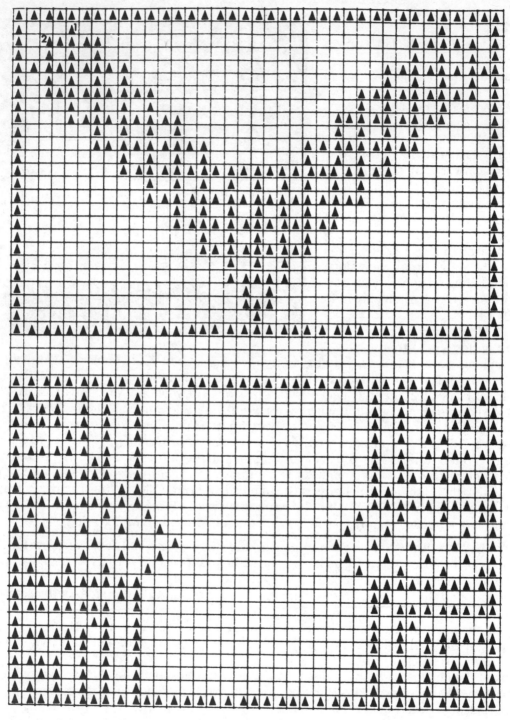

Design Charts

work the four stitches directly below #2. In other words, you can work in either direction. Just be sure to work one full stitch for each chart symbol.

Lining: The lining may be attached to each separate piece before joining or the lining can be seamed at all joinings and then attached just to the top edges of purse after separate pieces are joined. Cut each lining piece 1 inch longer and 1 inch wider than the corresponding canvas piece. Either make ½-inch seams at all points to be joined OR, if each piece of lining is to be attached separately, turn under and press in ½-inch seam allowances all around. Use a tiny whipping stitch to attach lining to canvas, catching stitches to the back of the needlepoint stitches.

Joining and Finishing: You are ready to join or finish the edges when stitching is completed and there is a single ridge or "thread" of canvas around all outer edges. Cover any edge that is not to be joined to another edge by using the overcast stitch. When two edges are to be joined, hold them so that wrong sides are facing each other and right sides are facing out. Line up the two pieces so that the holes of each piece are directly over each other. Then join them by using either the overcast stitch or the picot edging. If a single strand of yarn does not cover the edges adequately, use a double strand.

Order of Joining: There is no need to have any stitches on the bottom piece so it is ready to be joined when the stitching is finished on other pieces. If you have followed previous instructions, strap is joined to front and back pieces at center top. Now, join front, back, and two side pieces to bottom. Then, working from bottom to top, join front piece to each side piece and then join back piece to both side pieces. Finally, finish all top edges, using your choice of overcast, picot, or binding stitch.

"Terry's Picot Edging": Throughout the following instructions, the word "hole" will be used. However, when you are joining two pieces you will actually be working through one hole of each piece with each motion of the needle. To begin, secure yarn in previously worked stitches.

Stitch #1: Bring needle up in second hole from top.

Stitch #2: Take needle to back of work and bring it up in top hole.

Stitch #3: Take needle to back of work, skip over last two stitches made, skip over one empty hole, bring needle up in next empty hole.

Stitch #4: Take needle to back of work and bring it up in the empty hole you skipped when making stitch #3. Keep repeating stitches #3 and #4 until edge is covered or joined.

Overcast or Lacing: Bring needle up in first hole, take it to back of work and bring it up in second hole, take it to back of work and bring it up in third hole. Continue in this manner until edge is covered or joined.

With either method, at each corner, take an extra stitch or two as needed to neatly cover the corner.

Binding Stitch (see p. 18-20): Work over three stitches as for lacing stitch, then (A) go backwards two holes, bring needle up in that hole, then (B) go forward to next empty hole and bring needle up in that hole. Continue to repeat from A to B along edge.

TISSUE BOX COVERS

MATERIALS

Two sheets of 10-mesh plastic canvas

Knitting worsted or tapestry yarn—approximately 100 yards per box

(If two colors are to be used, plan for approximately 60 yards of each color.

If three colors are to be used, plan for approximately 40 yards of each color.)

#18 tapestry needle

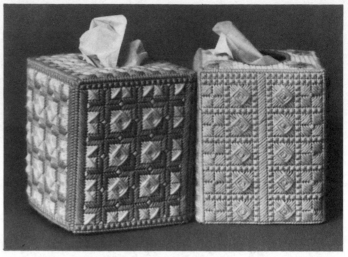

While traditional needlepoint canvas may be used, plastic canvas is recommended for all but those people who are experienced in construction principles. Persian or tapestry yarn may be used, but knitting-worsted acrylic yarn is quite satisfactory for this project—good news for knitters and crocheters who usually have lots of leftover yarns around.

The boxes may be made in solid colors (quite elegant this way) or in a combination of two or more colors.

The cutting dimensions given for the plastic canvas fit a Kleenex Boutique Tissue Box. If you are using other brands, you may find it necessary to make the side and top pieces slightly larger. Buy a box of tissues before cutting any of your canvas.

If the stitches used in making these boxes are not familiar to you, I suggest that you cut off a small piece of canvas and practice each of the stitches before beginning the box.

Cut four pieces of plastic canvas, each one having 43 holes across and 53 holes down, for the four sides of the box. Cut another piece with 43 holes in each direction for the top.

Note: With pieces this size, you will be working over 42 threads horizontally and 52 threads vertically. This thread count is given for those who may wish to plan a different pattern-stitch arrangement than the two shown here.

To work the two-toned box as shown, start at the upper left-hand corner and work a row of 21 Smyrna stitches across the top. Then, starting at the upper right-hand corner, count across to the fourth Smyrna stitch from this edge. Bring the needle up in this stitch in space marked with #5 on the Smyrna stitch chart. Consider this as Stitch #1 on the Coventry cross chart. Work a total of 12 Coventry crosses, having three in each horizontal pattern across and four in each vertical pattern down. (See photograph.) Next work a row of slanting Gobelin down each side. Next, work a waffle stitch in each 8-thread square (six in all) or fill these spaces with the stitch or stitches of your choice. Finally, fill the small squares and oblongs around the outer edges of the Coventry cross pattern with Scotch stitches. These may be slanted all in one direction or may slant toward each other. To do this, use half of the flat stitch chart. You may add another dimension to these Scotch stitches by "crossing" them, as I did on the two-toned tissue cover shown. To do this, refer

TISSUE BOX COVERS

Scotch Stitch

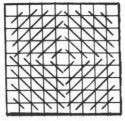

Flat Stitch

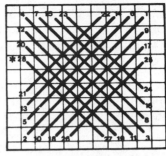

Waffle Stitch

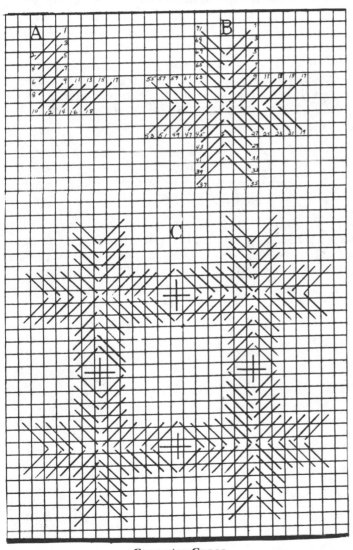

Coventry Cross

Rice Stitch

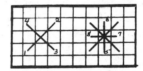

Smyrna Stitch

Mosaic Stitch

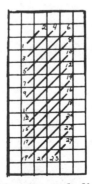

Slanting Gobelin

103

to the Scotch stitch chart and bring needle up at "a" and take it down at "b" —or bring it up at "b" and take it down at "a." When your Scotch stitch is worked in an opposing direction, this slanted stitch will also change direction. Finish by working a row of Smyrna stitch across the bottom.

The solid color box is worked with a slightly different arrangement of stitches. The Coventry cross is not used in this box, while the flat stitch has been added. Also, French knots were used in the center of each waffle stitch and each flat stitch. If you will study the flat stitch chart, you will see that it is composed of a set of four Scotch stitches, slanted in opposite directions. The slanting Gobelin shown down the center of this box is worked over two threads instead of over three threads as shown on the chart. In other words, each long stitch is only the length shown from #3 to #4 on that chart. After this photograph was made, I worked a solid color box with the same stitches arranged differently, which I prefer to the one shown. For this one, I worked one row of Smyrna stitches around each edge. Directly under the sixth Smyrna stitch from the upper right corner, I made a vertical row of Smyrna stitches from top to bottom. I did the same under the 11th and 16th Smyrna stitches from the same edge. Then I made horizontal Smyrna stitch rows in the sixth, 11th, 16th, and 21st stitches down from the top edge. This gave me 20 eight-thread squares, which I filled with waffle and flat stitches.

Many stitch combinations are beautiful—so let your imagination go and create your own original design! For the top of each box, you might try rows of mosaic stitch, leaving an unworked area approximately 1½-by-2 inches in the center of the top. Cut out this unworked space for the opening through which the tissues are pulled.

To join the pieces use an overcast or whipping stitch. Place two pieces together with right sides facing out. Carefully line up the edge holes and bring the needle up through matching holes—one on each piece. Then bring the needle up through the next two matching holes. Continue in this manner until the edge is covered and joined. For ease in working, I suggest that you first join each side piece to one edge of the top before joining the side pieces together. Then, working from top to bottom, join each side piece to the adjoining piece. Finally, overcast the edges of the top opening and all bottom edges.

PHONE BOOK COVERS

MATERIALS

Three Darice 7-mesh plastic canvas sheets (10½-by-13 inches each)

One 3½-ounce skein Wintuk hand-knitting yarn in knitting worsted-weight for background

One ⅓-ounce skein Wintuk hand-knitting yarn in each of following colors (or colors of your choice):

Flower Garden Design:

amethyst   blue jewel
yellow   sea coral
scarlet   turquoise
small amount light and dark green

Medallion Design:

wood brown
paddy green
whiskey gold
tangerine

Stiffening: Two cardboard strips, length of book and about 3 inches wide

Adhesive: Two strips of stitch witchery or other binding material cut the length of the book
Lining: ½-yard of fabric of your choice

Preparing Canvas: Cut two sections about ¼ inch larger than book to be covered. Cut one section the length and width of book binding.

Front: Select design to be worked and center on canvas. The center of the canvas is denoted on each chart with a solid black square. On the flower design this stitch is to be worked in the color used for the center flower. On the medallion design, it is to be worked in the color designated by this mark: /. The design and the background are to be worked in half-cross or continental stitch.

Back: The design is not repeated on the back. The back may be worked in half-cross, continental, or a decorative stitch. If you

wish to use a decorative stitch, count spaces in length of canvas and in width. If you have a multiple of three plus one, you can use the Scotch stitch, for example. With a multiple of two plus one, the mosaic stitch would be a good choice.

Color Code

● = gold

▲ = brown

╱ = green

✕ = tangerine

The solid square ■ denotes center of canvas and is worked in green.

Binding: Work in half-cross, continental, or the decorative stitch used on the back. If desired, the word "Telephone" or name of the recipient can be worked down binding if it is not on front.

Assembly: Using doubled yarn, lace the three pieces together. Then work around entire edge with double lacing of yarn.

Lining: Cut lining around open book cover. Cut approximately 3 inches wider than book and 10 inches longer. With book cover open on lining, place pieces of cardboard at edges of book. Fold balance of lining material over cardboard and secure with stitch witchery.

Fold stiffened edges over balance of lining that should now be same length as book being covered. Place inside book. Fold under top and bottom edges and tack to book.

Start First Stitch: Hold short end of yarn at back and work over end for several stitches. To end or begin new strands, weave yarn into wrong side of stitches previously worked. Do not tie knots.

For Even Stitches: If yarn becomes twisted while working, drop needle and allow to resume natural twist. Work stitches with a light, even tension so they lay evenly, covering plastic well.

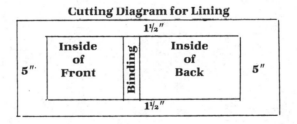

Cutting Diagram for Lining

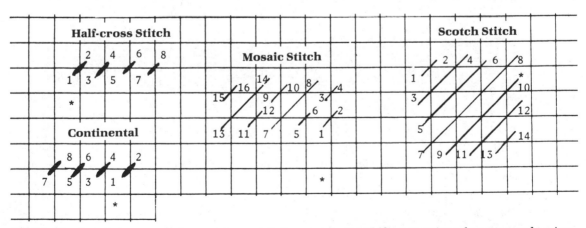

NOTE: Needle comes up at 1, down at 2, up at 3, down at 4, etc. *indicates point where second series of stitches is made.

Color Code: Each of the flowers above is numbered. The dots for each flower are worked in the corresponding number. The flower centers are filled with yellow stitches (except for the yellow flower, which should have a tangerine center). Design is most effective if the flower centers are worked in French knots.

Flower #1: scarlet
Flower #2: tangerine
Flower #3: yellow

Flower #4: blue jewel
Flower #5: sea coral
Flower #6: amethyst

Flower #7: tangerine
╱ = light green
╲ = dark green

MONOGRAM TOTE BAG

MATERIALS

Three sheets 7-mesh plastic canvas

Persian or Persian-type needlepoint yarn OR tapestry yarn OR 4-ply worsted-weight knitting yarn:

    36 yards of dark color

    96 yards of medium color

    160 yards of light color

#18 tapestry needle

½-yard lining fabric (optional)

Cutting the Canvas: The front and back pieces of the tote bag as shown measure about 8-inches square and cutting directions will be for a bag that size. It can be made larger by adding additional Smyrna stitch borders. Each additional row (worked around all edges) will make the bag approximately ½ inch wider and ½ inch taller.

For the front and back sections for an 8-inch bag, cut two pieces each having 57 holes in each direction. (Add four holes in each direction for each size larger.)

For the two side panels cut two pieces, each having 19 holes across and 57 holes down. (Make pieces four holes longer for each size larger.) For bottom panel, cut one piece 19 holes by 57, adding the extra four holes to length of piece for each size larger. For handle (regardless of bag size) cut two pieces, each having 31 holes by 11 holes.

Working the Pattern Stitches: For each pattern stitch, unless you are instructed otherwise, bring your needle up from the wrong side to the right side at each odd number and take it down from the right side to the wrong side at even numbers. In other words, bring needle up at #1; take needle down at #2; bring needle up at #3; take needle down at #4.

If you are a beginner, I suggest that you practice each of the stitches shown on a scrap of canvas. You will be surprised and delighted to see how easily you can achieve dramatic effects with decorative stitches.

Adjoining Stitches: The accompanying stitch charts show how adjoining stitches "share" holes. To practice, work a vertical row of Smyrna stitches, beginning in the upper left corner of a scrap piece of canvas. First, follow the four steps shown in Smyrna stitch diagram (Chart C). To make the second Smyrna stitch (Chart D), count down two holes from the point where first stitch was started (hole #1) and bring needle up in that hole. Take needle down in hole where second part of the original Smyrna stitch was made (hole #3).

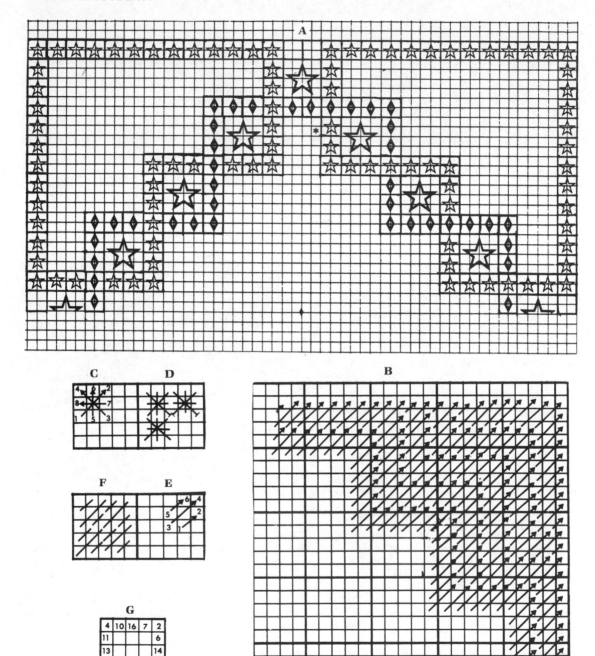

You have now taken the first step in making your second Smyrna stitch. Continue by following numbers 3 through 8. Practice the other stitches shown in similar fashion. Lines showing stitch direction are not included on Rhodes stitch diagram (Chart G) as it was felt that the criss-crossing of so many lines would be confusing rather than helpful.

Design Chart: Chart A shows the top half of the complete design. To work the bottom half, turn chart upside down and work down. Each small square represents one Smyrna stitch. The ones with small stars are worked in the medium color; the ones with diamonds are done in the dark color; and blank squares are worked in the light color.

Each of the squares containing large stars represents one Rhodes stitch worked in the light color.

Note: If you are making bag larger, work extra row(s) around outer edges in Smyrna stitch using medium color.

The blank areas in each corner are to be worked in the zigzag stitch with light color. The zigzag stitch diagram (Chart B) shows how the upper right corner is worked. Other corners are worked in the same manner, with the stitch direction reversed for upper left and lower right corners. Balance of design is to be worked in mosaic stitch (Charts E and F).

After all Smyrna, Rhodes, and zigzag stitches have been worked, select the initial you wish from monogram chart shown and see directions for working initial.

Handles: Overlap two short ends of the two handle pieces for about eight holes. Work four rows of Smyrna stitches, working through both thicknesses, thus joining the two pieces. Next, work rows of Smyrna stitch in each direction from these center four rows to within about four rows from each end. Place the unworked end of one end of handle under the top of one side piece. Then as you work the top rows of side piece, pass needle through both thicknesses, thus joining handle to side piece. Do the same on the other side.

Sides and Bottom of Bag: Work one row of Smyrna stitch, medium color, around all outer edges, filling in center of each piece with mosaic stitch in light color.

Optional Lining: Cut fabric pieces 1 inch wider and 1 inch longer than each piece (except handle which is not lined). Fold under and press a ½-inch hem on each piece and whip each lining piece to the matching needlepointed piece a fraction of an inch in from each edge.

To join pieces, hold two pieces together with right sides out. Pass needle through both thicknesses, from back to front, matching holes of one piece to holes of other piece. Take needle to back of work and pass through next pair of holes, thereby joining the work and finishing the edges at the same time. This is called overcasting.

First join the bottom edge of front to bottom piece then join back and two sides in same manner. Next, working from bottom to top, join side edges of all pieces.

Overcast all unfinished edges using same technique as used in joining but working through one thickness only.

Working Monogram: Starting at point marked with * (near upper center portion of design chart), work seven rows of mosaic stitch. Start the top row of the desired initial on next row, centering the initial on this row. The needle-pointer with some experience will find that some parts of each initial can be worked in mosaic stitch, but the beginner will probably find it easier to work entire initial in tent stitch. (One tent stitch is worked by following Step 1-2 in mosaic stitch.) Fill in remaining portion of unworked area with mosaic stitch, making single tent stitches where necessary around initial to keep in pattern.

CARDINAL WASTEBASKET COVER

MATERIALS

Three Darice 7-mesh plastic canvas sheets (10½-by-13 inches each)

4-ply knitting worsted-weight Wintuk yarn:

    7 ounces white or off white for background

    3 ounces bright red

    1 ounce light red

    1 ounce brown

    1 ounce dark green

    1 ounce medium green

    10 yards black

    2 yards gold

#14 tapestry needle

One oval wastebasket, approximately 13 inches high and 29 inches in circumference. Select a wastebasket that measures the same around top and bottom rather than one with sloping sides.

Cutting the Canvas: Hold the canvas up to the wastebasket and cut one sheet so that it is the same height as the wastebasket. Now trim off one edge so that it is 11 inches wide. Cut a second sheet to the same measurements. This will give you the front and the back pieces. From the third sheet of canvas, cut two side sections. Each of these sections should be the same height as the back and front pieces and as wide as needed to make the cover fit the wastebasket. To find the accurate width for these pieces, secure the front and back pieces to the wastebasket with a large rubber band. Now measure the space between front and back on each side. Wherever you have cut the plastic, trim off all "nubs" along the cut edges so that all edges are smooth.

Following the Chart: Each square of the graph chart represents one stitch worked in the color denoted by the symbol in that square. All blank squares are worked in the background color. Work in continental stitch throughout. In the chart you will find, on the body of the cardinal, one square that has a black dot with a circle around it. This is the exact center of the design. Find the center of your canvas, vertically and horizontally. Mark the center vertical line and the center horizontal line with a basting thread. The point where these threads cross will be the exact center. Thread your needle with red, count over seven holes to the right from the center, and take one stitch at that point. Working from right to left, make 17 stitches in red. If you are not accustomed to working from charts, you may find it helpful to make a check mark by each row as you complete it. I

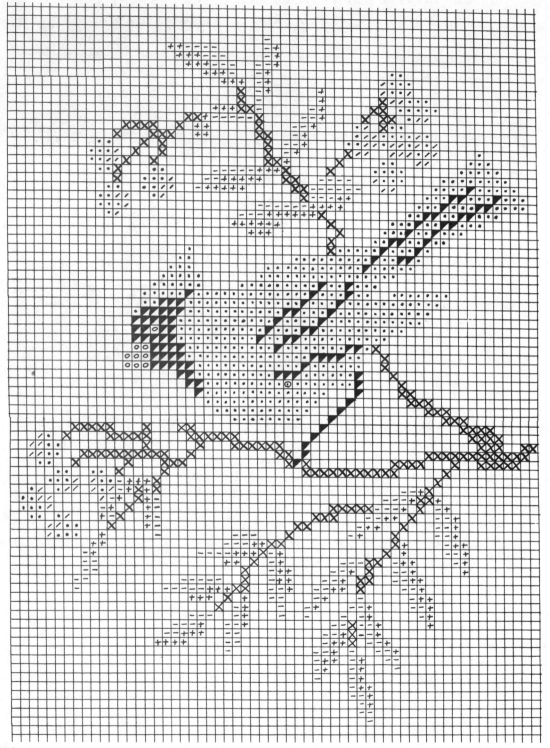

would suggest that you then continue working down, until the bottom five rows of the cardinal's body have been completed. Next, you might wish to turn the chart and the canvas upside down and finish stitching the cardinal before starting on the branches, leaves, and berries. After you have completed the design, you may wish to make a border of two rows of brown at the top and bottom edge of the piece. Finally, fill in the background. Make another piece in the same manner. Then work two side pieces, following the chart at right. Again, a circle marks the center of the chart. Start with brown, one stitch below and to the left of the center.

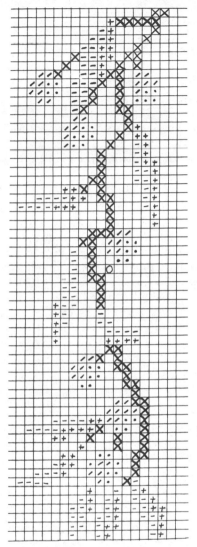

Chart for Side Section

 = bright red

= light red

= brown

= black

= dark green

= light green

= gold

INDIAN MOTIF TOTE OR PILLOW

MATERIALS

Coats & Clark's Red Heart "Wintuk" hand-knitting yarn (knitting worsted-weight)

    Color A: 160 yards
    Color B: 80 yards
    Color C: 80 yards
    Color D: 24 yards

(Yardages are approximate and are for both sides of pillow or tote. If you want one side to be made of fabric, you will require only half as much yarn.)

#18 tapestry needle

10-mesh plastic canvas: two 17-inch-square pieces. Finished sizes of bag or pillow will be approximately 15-by-16½ inches. While seam allowances are unnecessary, it is advisable to purchase slightly wider pieces than needed as mesh-count might vary from one manufacturer to another.

Cotton or polyester mono canvas can be used, allowing an extra inch all around for seam allowances. With either of these, you may want to use some form of stiffening for the bag.

Lining: ½-yard fabric

To Work Design: All stitches are worked over four threads or ribs of canvas. Each symbol on the design chart represents a block of four stitches, as illustrated in the small chart. For each stitch, bring needle up in a numbered square (which represents a hole in the canvas) and take needle down at tip of arrow four threads directly above it. If you follow the illustration, starting at number 1, you will be working from left to right. If you prefer, you can start at number 4 and work from right to left. You have a choice of starting at the center and working out in all directions from the center (vertical and horizontal centers are marked with arrows on the design chart) or you can start in upper right or left corners of the design. Remember that every chart symbol represents four stitches!

PLASTIC CANVAS

Joining Pieces: If plastic canvas is used, no hemming or blocking is necessary; simply trim away excess canvas, leaving just one rib of canvas around all edges. Place the two pieces together with wrong sides together and right sides facing out and whip together along three sides. For Pillow: At this point, insert pillow form and then whip together the remaining side. If you cannot find a pillow form the correct size, you can make one by cutting fabric 1 inch larger than each needlepoint piece in each direction;

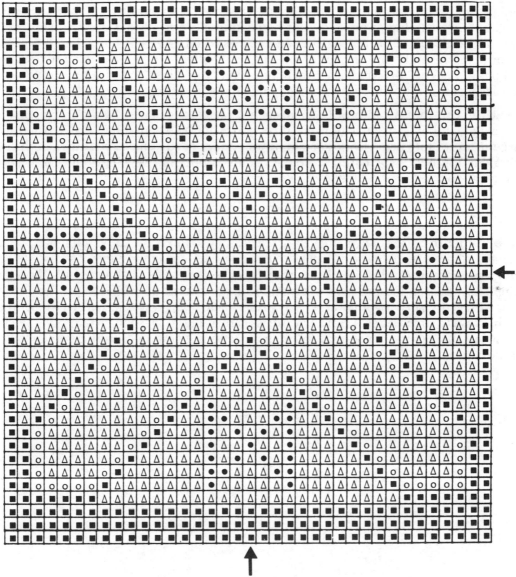

Color Code and Suggested Color Combinations

■	Color A	coffee	navy	black
●	Color B	bronze	red	turquoise
△	Color C	beige	light blue	eggshell
○	Color D	burnt orange	emerald	gray

Note: In each combination, Color C is the background color. You may, of course, use any color of your choice for any of those listed above.

joining the two pieces on three sides; stuffing it with cotton or polyester stuffing; and then sewing the remaining seam. Sew cording around all four sides if desired. For Tote Bag: Overcast top edge of each piece. Cut two pieces of fabric, each 1 inch longer and 1 inch wider than finished front or back of tote bag. Join with a ½-inch seam along two side edges and bottom edge. Turn under a ½-inch hem along top edges. Whip-stitch top of lining to tote bag just under the overcast stitches along top edge of bag.

Cording: Cut four strands of Color B, each 6 yards long. Twist lightly in one direction. Fold in half and twist again in opposite direction. Knot free ends. Sew cord in place around three seams of tote bag. Divide remaining amount of cord in half and sew to both sides of bag along top edges for handles. Note: Cording is optional on pillow, but can be sewed around all four edges if desired.

MONO CANVAS

Before Joining Pieces: You may find it necessary to block the canvas. If it has pulled out of shape, dampen each piece and pin it to a padded surface to the correct shape. Be sure to use rustproof pins and place pins in the unworked margins of the canvas. Allow to dry completely. Before joining pieces, machine-stitch around all edges to prevent raveling. Now, with right sides together and wrong sides facing out, sew the two pieces together by machine along three sides. Trim away excess canvas and turn so that right sides are facing out. From this point on, you may follow instructions given for finishing tote or pillow in plastic canvas.

LEARN-A-STITCH TOTE II

MATERIALS

Three Darice 7-mesh plastic canvas sheets (10½-by-13 inches each)

Acrylic yarn in 4-ply knitting worsted-weight as follows:

 Color A (background) white, ecru, or pale shade: one skein (3½ ounces)

 Color B (handle and borders) medium shade: one skein (3½ ounces)

 Color C (center design) darker shade: 20 yards

 Color D (center accent) green: 4 yards

#14 tapestry needle

½-yard 36-inch fabric for lining

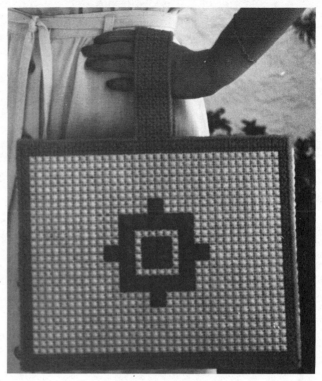

Cut plastic canvas so that you have:

Two pieces, each 77 holes across and 61 holes down for front and back of tote

Two pieces, each 13 holes across and 61 holes down for sides of tote

One piece, 77 holes across and 13 holes down for bottom of tote

One piece, 77 holes across and 9 holes down for handle of tote

SUGGESTED WORKING ORDER

Handle: Using Color B and, leaving three rows of unworked holes at each end of handle, work 30 rows consisting of four rice stitches per row. Overcast both long edges. Cut one piece of lining fabric 1 inch longer and 1 inch wider than handle. Set aside.

Panels: With Color B, work one row of rice stitch around all four sides of bottom panel and two side panels. Finish these panels by filling in with 28 rows with each row having four Smyrna stitches. The Smyrna stitches are worked with Color A.

Front of Tote: A "Coventry cross" or eight-pointed star (see p. 46 in the stitch chart section) is worked in the very center of the front and back section. Find the center hole of the canvas by first counting down from the top 31 holes. Run a basting thread through this 31st row of holes. Now count in 39 holes from one side edge and run a basting thread through this 39th row of holes. Where the basting threads meet is the center hole. Use Color C for the star. Then, with Color D, make a Smyrna stitch at each corner of the star and fill in the four small Vs at each side and top and bottom of the star with small slanting stitches.

119

Center: With Color A, work one row of Smyrna stitches around the square center motif.

A border of leviathan stitches is worked around the center motif, using Color C.

With Color B, work a border of rice stitches all around each edge of front and back of tote, except leave unworked a space for four rice stitches at the center top of each of these pieces. This is the space where the handles will be joined to the front and to the back of tote. In joining the handles you will work through both thicknesses of canvas. This will not be done, however, until the background of both pieces is finished for greater ease in handling.

Fill in all of background with Smyrna stitches worked in Color A.

Make a second piece identical to the front for the back piece of your tote, unless you would like to be creative and work out a different design for the back. If you do work a different design on the back, I suggest that you carry out the rice stitch border on this piece as on all others.

BARGELLO PURSE

MATERIALS

Two sheets 10-mesh plastic canvas, each 10½-by-13 inches

Yarn:

    Color A = 90 yards
    Color B = 40 yards
    Color C = 40 yards
    Color D = 30 yards

The pocketbook, as shown, was made with pure wool Persian-type yarn. You may substitute tapestry yarn or knitting worsted-weight yarn, if you prefer.

Sample color combinations:

A— yellow	A— lavender
B— turquoise	B— pink
C— white	C— white
D— shamrock green	D— deep lavender
A— dark melon	A— light blue
B— deep salmon	B— marine blue
C— light peach	C— white
D— brown	D— deep blue

Two 6-inch rings for handles

#18 tapestry needle

¼-yard of fabric for lining

Cutting the Canvas: Cut two pieces—each measuring 9-by-12 inches. After doing this, you should have a narrow strip of canvas left over. From this, cut two small strips, each with four holes across and 31 holes down. These strips are used to fasten the ring handles to the purse. Trim edges on all pieces so that all edges are smooth.

Yarn: It is suggested that you cut yarn into approximately 30-inch lengths. If you are using the Persian-type yarn, always separate the three loosely twisted strands and lay them side by side before threading the needle. With any type of yarn, do not allow the yarn to become twisted as you work. To avoid twisting, give your needle a little counterclockwise turn after every two or three stitches. Occasionally let the needle hang free and the yarn will untwist itself.

Getting Started: Leaving three rows of holes unworked at each end, work five Scotch stitches on each of the small strips you cut for fastening handles. Use Color A for this and with same color, overcast the edges of these strips. Set aside.

Special Tip: When doing Bargello on plastic canvas, work one vertical row of continental stitch along each side edge before starting pattern, using color that will be used for joining

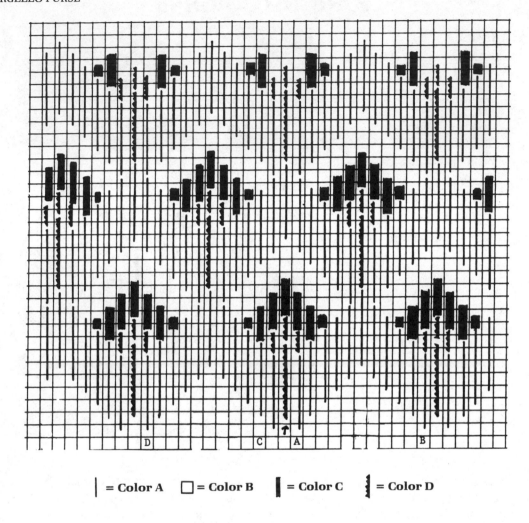

| = Color A   ☐ = Color B   ▌ = Color C   ⦚ = Color D

and finishing all edges. This makes it easier to join these edges. It is not necessary on top and bottom edges.

The center stitch of the bottom row is marked with a small black arrow. Find the center hole on your canvas by folding canvas piece in half. For the first stitch, with Color A, bring the needle up one hole to the right of the center. With the tip of your needle, count up six canvas "threads" or ribs and take needle down in next hole. This stitch will cover five holes and six threads. (Each line of the chart represents a canvas thread and each blank square represents one hole.) Next, bring needle up one hole above point where first stitch was started and take it down one hole above point where first stitch ended. Work from right to left. Continue making stitches in this manner—each stitch one hole above last one made— until you have six stitches completed. Now, start down by making each stitch one hole below last one made. When you have five stitches on each side of the center stitch, you will have completed one pattern repeat of this row (from A to B). Now, skip one vertical row of holes and work another pattern repeat. Continue in this manner until you reach the right-side edge. Then start one stitch to the left of the center row of holes and work to left-side edge, repeating from C to D as you go across. Remember to skip one row of holes between each pattern repeat.

Next, thread needle with Color D. Notice that the first stitch with Color D is made in the space left between each pattern repeat of the first row and that this stitch starts one hole up from the stitches on either side of it and finishes one hole higher. When this stitch is finished, make the short stitches on either side and above it. Note that each of these stitches covers two threads and one hole. Work all of the Color D stitches across the row. Then, work the Color C stitches in each pattern repeat and, finally, work the Color B stitches of each pattern repeat. Work all remaining rows in same manner following the chart.

Finishing: Before working last row of pattern, loop one of the strips worked in Scotch stitch over one of the ring handles. Baste the unworked ends of the strip to the top center edge of the pocketbook piece. As you work the pattern repeat for this top row, work through all three thicknesses of canvas, thus securing the handle strip to the pocketbook. Be sure that the ring is in place before you do this stitching. Complete final row of pattern. With Color A, fill in all remaining spaces at top and bottom.

Work the second piece in the same manner. Overcast top edges of both pieces. Cut two pieces of fabric 1 inch wider and 1 inch longer than each needlepointed piece. Turn under a ½-inch seam allowance on all edges of fabric and press. With sewing thread, whip lining in place on each piece.

Place the front and back of pocketbook together with wrong sides together and right sides facing out. Overcast the sides and the bottom edges together.

FROST FANTASIES

MATERIALS

Red and green 7-mesh plastic canvas (one sheet will make approximately six to eight ornaments)

Knitting worsted-weight yarn or tapestry yarn—large ornaments take 5 yards of white and 2 yards of trim color; small ornaments take 3 yards white and 1½ yards for trim; candy canes take 2 yards white and 1½ yards for trim (yardages are approximate)

#18 tapestry needle

Cutting Directions: Use the charts as a cutting guide. Be sure to cut outside the bold dark lines letting those lines represent the outside ribs of canvas. Trim all edges so that they are smooth. To avoid extra counting and measuring, cut one of each shape and then use that one as a pattern for cutting others.

Instructions: Using white yarn, work the design on one side of each shape. It is not necessary to use any background stitches—just let the colored canvas show. Be careful not to carry yarn across blank areas of the canvas. When starting a new strand of yarn, leave a 3-inch tail hanging; when the pattern stitch is complete, you can then weave this tail end under the stitches just worked. When you finish a pattern stitch area, weave the finishing tail end of yarn under stitches just worked also. Clip all ends close to work as soon as they are secured.

Stitch Chart Notes: The lines on the charts represent "ribs" or "threads" of the canvas. The blank squares represent the holes in the canvas.

The needle is always brought up in a numbered hole (starting with #1 and continuing through other numbers, in order) and is taken down either at the point of an arrow or where a circle or square appears. (Circles and squares are used where several stitches share a canvas hole.)

Charts A, B, and C show details for three of the pattern stitches. Chart A is for the Rhodes stitch, starting with a large cross-stitch. The second box of Chart A shows the third and fourth steps, while the third box shows the final steps. Chart B shows the sequence of stitches for the Smyrna stitch. Chart C shows details of the mandarin stitch.

Ornament No. 1: In each corner, make a Rhodes stitch. The chart shows one corner fully charted, while only the first two steps of the pattern are shown for the other corners (see

124

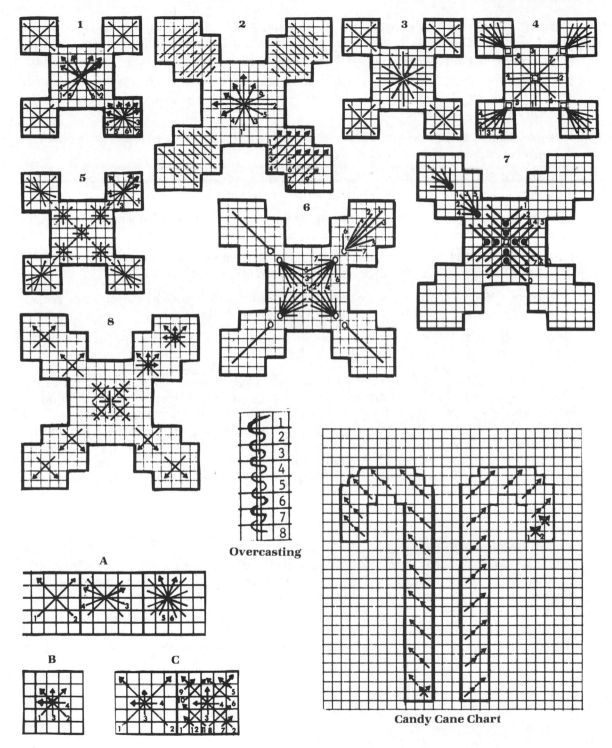

Overcasting

A

B

C

Candy Cane Chart

Chart A). The center of this ornament uses a triple-cross stitch. Bring needle up at #1 and take it down at the point of the arrow in upper right corner. Continue in this manner, bringing needle up at numbers and taking it down at arrow points.

Ornament No. 2: The center is worked in a diamond cross-stitch, while the corners are done in Milanese stitch. Just follow the numbers and arrows as instructed in Stitch Chart Notes.

Ornament No. 3: The center is a diamond cross-stitch worked the same as in Ornament 2. Work corners in Smyrna stitch (Chart B).

Ornament No. 4: The center is star stitch, with ray stitches worked in the corners. See Stitch Chart Notes for explanation of the square symbols.

Ornament No. 5: Work five Smyrna stitches in center and follow chart in upper right corner for tied crosses. Work all corners the same.

Ornament No. 6: Long leaf stitches are used in each corner with short leaf stitches used in center. Only one corner is fully charted, but each is worked the same.

Ornament No. 7: Work eight-pointed star in center with two short ray stitches in each corner. Only one corner is fully charted but each is worked the same.

Ornament No. 8: Work two Smyrna stitches in each corner with a mandarin stitch in the center. See stitch Chart C for mandarin stitch detail.

Candy Canes: See the Candy Cane Chart. Notice that there are two charts for the canes. It is necessary to work back and front so that the crook of the canes are in opposite directions. The candy canes are worked with simple cross-stitches. Look at the tip of the crook of the right cane. Bring needle up in hole marked "1," take it down at tip of arrow, bring it up at "2," and again down at arrow point. One cross-stitch is now completed. Notice that one more cross-stitch is charted just above and to the right of the first. Balance of candy cane is charted with only half of each cross-stitch shown but you are to make a full cross-stitch wherever an arrow appears.

Follow finishing directions below.

Finishing: Work two pieces for each ornament. Join the two together having right sides out. Hold two matching pieces together and, with yarn the same color as the canvas, join them with a simple overcasting stitch. To do this, bring needle up through matching holes of each piece; pass needle to back of work and again bring needle up through the next set of holes. Continue around until all edges are joined, leaving a loop of yarn free at one corner for a hanger. If you prefer, you can work through every other set of holes. Also, it is not necessary to work extra stitches in the corners for complete coverage when your yarn color matches your canvas color.

NEEDLEPOINT ORNAMENTS

MATERIALS

10-mesh plastic canvas: Two 10½-by-13-inch sheets will make one of each ornament shown (for a total of 5 ornaments)

10-mesh regular canvas: One strip 10-by-29 inches will make the same number of ornaments (The additional canvas is needed as a 1½-inch unworked margin must be allowed around all edges for blocking.)

Tapestry or Persian yarn: Quantities given are sufficient for five ornaments (one each):

red:	17 yards
white:	33 yards
green:	45 yards
black:	10 yards
flesh:	4½ yards
blue:	1 yard

Backing: One strip of felt, 6½-by-18 inches

Working Instructions

Cutting Canvas: The instructions that follow are for plastic canvas that will need no blocking and no "turn-under." If you are using regular needlepoint canvas, add 1½ inches on each of the four sides for each piece.

Cut one piece of canvas for each ornament having the number of holes given for each one as follows:

tree = 33 holes by 56 holes	snowman = 29 holes by 60 holes
bells = 26 holes by 65 holes	soldier = 28 holes by 64 holes

Santa Claus = 30 holes by 60 holes

Trim each piece so that all edges are smooth.

Following Chart: Each square of the graph chart represents one stitch. Each symbol on the chart represents a stitch in the color denoted by that symbol. For example, wherever you see an x on the chart, make a single stitch in gold. If you have never worked needlepoint following a chart before, I suggest that you start with the snowman. Starting at the upper right-hand corner, using the continental stitch, work two full rows of green. Then, on the third row down, work 16 stitches in green, eight stitches in red, and four stitches in green. You have now worked the first row of the snowman's hat. Continue working down, making a stitch in the proper color for each square of the graph.

Stitches: You may use basketweave, half-cross, or continental stitch. On the plastic canvas, I recommend that you use the continental stitch, working horizontally. Bring the needle up at #1, take it down at #2, bring it up at #3, take it down at #4. Continue in this manner, always coming up at odd numbers and going down at even numbers. More experienced needlepointers may prefer to use some pattern stitches to add extra interest. A diagram is given for "turkey work," which, when used for Santa's beard, gives a loopy texture. French knots are effectively used for buttons on the three figures. If you have never done "turkey work," I suggest that you try this stitch on a scrap of canvas. If this is to be used, I recommend that you do all of the design except for the hair and beard. Then work these last, starting at the bottom of the beard and working up.

Finishing: One of the primary reasons for using plastic canvas is the ease in finishing. When you have completed the needlepoint stitches, you need only to overcast the edges. To do this, bring the needle up in one edge stitch, then bring it up in the next stitch, allowing the yarn to cover the edge as you do so. At the top center of each ornament, leave a loop of yarn for hanging the ornament on the tree. Cut a piece of felt in the exact shape of the ornament and glue to the wrong side of ornament. If you are using regular needlepoint canvas, you will need to block the pieces if they have pulled out of shape and allow to dry completely. Then, trim away part of the excess canvas, leaving about ½ inch on each side, top and bottom. Turn this under, mitering corners, and glue or slip-stitch in place. Work binding stitch around all edges, making a loop at top center. With this type of canvas, you may also need to place a piece of heavy cardboard between the needlepoint and the backing for extra stiffness.

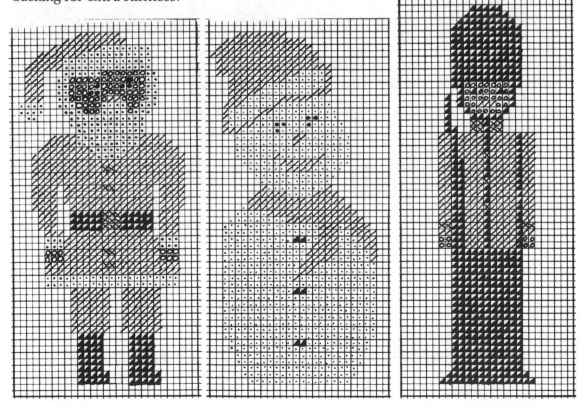

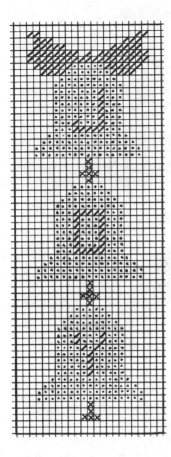

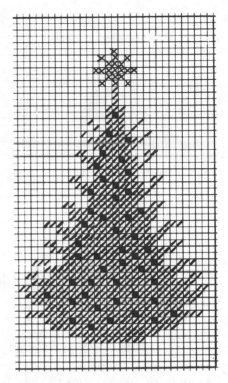

Color Code for Christmas Tree:

The / symbols stand for stitches worked in green. Solid color squares are worked in gold or in a variety of colors as you desire. A white background with a one-stitch border of green is used for this design.

Color Code:

(use for Santa, snowman, soldier, and bells)

All blank squares are worked in green.

- ╱ = red
- · = white
- ◢ = black
- x = gold
- o = flesh
- ● = blue

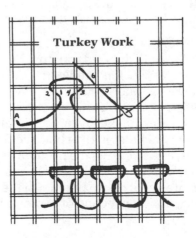

129

FROST FLOWER ORNAMENTS

MATERIALS

Red and green plastic canvas sheets (10½-by-13 inches—one sheet makes six ornaments)

Approximately 6 yards white acrylic yarn (4-ply) for each ornament

#18 tapestry needle

Design Identification Chart

```
            #1
        #2      #3
      #4    #5    #6
   #7   #8   #9   #10   #11
        #12
```

The horizontal and vertical double lines on the charts represent the plastic ribs that are called "canvas threads" in the instructions. The point where a horizontal and vertical "thread" cross over one another is called a "mesh." To determine how large to cut a square, allow one hole for each blank square on the chart. For example, there are 15 squares in each direction for Design #1. Cut the canvas so that you have 15 holes in each direction. Count carefully for each design before cutting canvas for that design.

Cut two squares for each ornament. Work design on one side of each. Hold two squares together with wrong sides facing each other. Whip the two pieces together going into every other hole around all four edges, leaving a ½-inch loop of yarn where you wish to have the hanger.

Be sure to weave in all loose ends of yarn on wrong side and take care not to carry yarn across blank areas of canvas. Do not use any background stitches—just let the colored canvas show. When cutting canvas squares, trim all edges so they are smooth.

Design #1: Start with ray stitch in upper left corner. In the second vertical row of holes, bring needle up in fifth hole from top. Take needle down in second hole from top in same row (Step 1-2). Now bring needle up in Hole #3 and take it down in same hole as before. Continue in this manner, bringing needle up at odd numbers and taking needle down in same hole each time. Work a ray stitch in each corner in same way. Next, start center design by first working the inverted triangle shown in center of diagram (⋀). Bring needle up in center row of holes in fifth hole from top (#1), take it down in second hole from top in same vertical row; bring needle up at #3, take it down in same hole as before; bring needle up at #5 and take it down in same hole as before. Now bring needle up again at #1 and take it down in center hole of ornament. Do the same at #3 and #5. *Rotate canvas one-quarter turn and work another section of center design in same manner.* Repeat from * to * twice more.

Design #2: Start by bringing needle up in sixth hole from right edge in second row of holes; take it down in next to last hole of this row. Now, bring needle up in hole marked #3 and take it down in same hole as before. Do the same with Steps 5, 7, 9 (open ray stitch). Work an open ray stitch in same manner in each corner. Start the 8-pointed star stitch by bringing needle up in eighth hole from right edge in fourth row from top (#1). Take it down in center hole two rows below. Note that you cross two meshes and one empty hole. Continue in this way, bringing needle up in each odd-numbered hole and taking it down as shown on chart.

Design #3: Start in upper left corner and bring needle up in second hole from top (#1), cross one mesh diagonally, and take needle down in second hole from left in top row of holes (#2). Now, following chart, bring needle up at odd numbers and take needle down at even numbers until you have completed steps 25-26 (Milanese stitch). *Rotate canvas one-quarter turn and work Milanese stitch in next corner.* Repeat from * to * twice more. Now, work one tied cross-stitch in center, again bringing needle up at odd numbers and taking it down at even numbers.

Design #4: Find the center hole of the canvas and bring needle up one hole below center hole (#1); take needle down in second hole above, now bring needle up at #3 and take down at #4, thus making the upright cross-stitch in center. From Hole #2 of this cross-stitch, count across to the fourth empty hole to the right of #2. Start first ray stitch here. (See ray stitch instructions in Design #1.) Finally, work four tied cross-stitches (see instructions in Design #3), placing them as shown in chart for Design #4.

Design #5: Start with the tied-windmill stitch in the center. Bring needle up in center hole of third row of holes from bottom (#1) and take it down in center hole of third row from top (#2). Continue by bringing needle up at #3, down at #4, up at #5, down at #6, up at #7, down at #8, up at #9, down at #10. The surrounding stitches are tied-wheat stitches. To do these, first make four vertical stitches as shown in upper right of chart. Then, bring needle up at dot in second row below #3, taking care not to pass needle through any part of the stitch. If necessary, hold the stitch to one side with your thumbnail. Now, pass needle under the two stitches to the left of dot, bring yarn forward and pass it over all four vertical stitches. Again, taking care not to catch needle in any stitch, insert needle where the dot appears under #5, passing needle under Stitches 5 and 7. Make three more tied-wheat stitches in same manner, placing them as shown on chart.

Design #6: This design is entirely made up of Smyrna stitches. All steps of this stitch cross over two canvas threads and one hole. First, a diagonal stitch is taken from 1 to 2; another diagonal stitch is then taken from 3 to 4 (cross-stitch made); then a vertical straight stitch is taken from 5 to 6; followed by a horizontal straight stitch from 7 to 8, thus completing one Smyrna stitch. Only the center stitch has numbered stitches, but all others are worked in same way. Start first stitch in hole marked "A," which is five holes down from top and nine holes in from right edge. Follow chart for placement of each Smyrna stitch.

Design #7: To begin this design, make a small cross-stitch in the center of the canvas square. Then make the larger cross-stitches above, below, and to the sides of the center cross-stitch. Then fill in with the straight stitches shown in this center design motif. In each

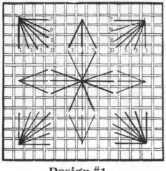

Design #1

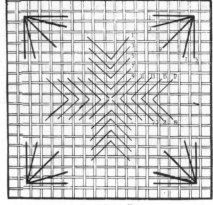

Design #2

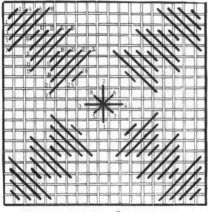

Design #3

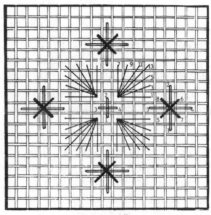

Design #4

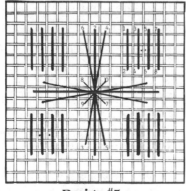

Design #5

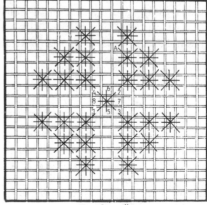

Design #6

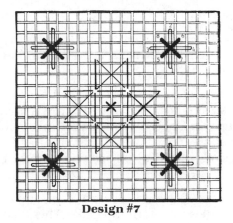

Design #7

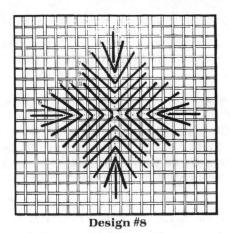

Design #8

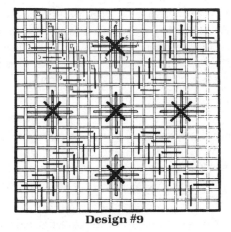

Design #9

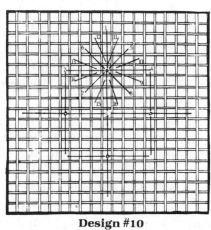

Design #10

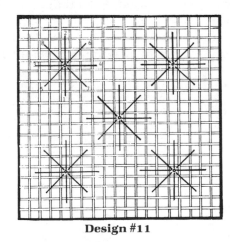

Design #11

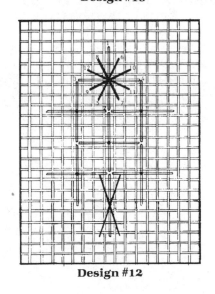

Design #12

corner, make a tied cross-stitch as described in Design #3.

Design #8: Bring needle up at #1, take it over two holes and three canvas threads to the point shown by a dot. Next, bring needle up at #3 and take it down at second dot. Continue in this manner all around working in a counterclockwise direction.

Design #9: *Start in upper left corner in third hole from top at #1. Cross two threads and one hole. Continue taking the same length horizontal stitches each one hole closer to the center than the preceding stitch (at #s 3, 5, 7, 9, and 11). Then make the vertical stitches starting at #13.* Rotate canvas one-quarter turn and repeat from * to * until all four corner sections are worked. Then work five tied-cross stitches (see directions in Design #3), placing them as shown on chart.

Design #10: Bring needle up in hole #1 (the center hole of second row from top) and take it down in fourth hole below, passing over three holes and four threads. This hole is marked with a small circle on chart. Next, bring needle up at #2 and take it down in same hole with first stitch. Do the same for stitches #3 through #8, also taking needle down in same hole as first stitch. Now, take Stitches 9 through 16, noticing that these stitches do not end in the center stitch, but one hole to the side or below the center. When the 16th stitch is completed, you have one diamond eyelet stitch. Three more diamond eyelets are to be made, but only the first four stitches of each of these are charted. Work each in same manner as first.

Design #11: Bring needle up in Hole #1 (five holes in from left edge and eight holes down from top). Skip over three holes and four threads, taking needle down in hole marked with small circle. Bring needle up in Hole #2 and take it down in hole where first stitch ended. Continue around in this way, ending each stitch in same hole. Star stitch is complete after Step #8. Make four more star stitches, placing them as shown on chart. Only the first four stitches are shown for each of the remaining star stitches.

Design #12: Bring needle up in Hole #1 (three holes down from top in center vertical row of holes). Skip over five holes and six threads, taking needle down at #2. Continue around, bringing needle up at odd numbers and taking needle down at even numbers. Make five more flower cross-stitches in same manner, placing them as shown on chart. Only the first two stitches are shown for each remaining flower cross-stitch. Complete design by working the stem cross shown at bottom.

PLASTIC POINT MOBILES

MATERIALS

Red or green 7-mesh plastic canvas—one sheet for each Noel mobile and one sheet for each snowman

4-ply knitting yarn:

For Noel:
  30 yards white
    8 yards red or green

For snowman:
  40 yards white
    3 yards color of choice for hat, eyes, and buttons

Plastic rings, 7/8-inch or 1-inch size—four for each Noel

#18 tapestry needle

Noel Mobile: Work two squares for each letter. With right sides together, whip together the two squares for each letter.

When overcasting along the top edges of each square, work the three center stitches over plastic rings, thus securing them to square. When overcasting the "L" square, secure tassel to bottom edge in same manner.

Tassel: Cut a piece of cardboard 4 inches long. Wind yarn 30 times around cardboard. Cut a 4-inch or 5-inch strand of yarn and slide it under yarn at top of cardboard. Tie this strand tightly around all strands. Cut all strands at opposite end. Cut another piece of yarn and tie tightly several times around tassel 1 inch down from top. Knot, and let ends hang as part of tassel.

Tree Ornaments: From leftover canvas, you can make tree ornaments. Some suggested designs are shown on the Tree Ornaments Chart. Finish these just as you do for the Noel letters, except just make a loop of yarn for the hanger on top edge.

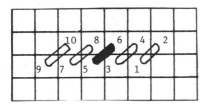

Figure A

Noel Decorations

For one Noel mobile or banner, cut eight squares of canvas, each having 20 holes in each direction. All of the lettering is done in continental stitch as shown in Figure A. To start the letter "N," beginning in upper right corner of one square, count down to fourth hole from top and fourth hole in from right edge. Bring needle up at this point, which is #1 in Figure A. Cross diagonally over one mesh and take needle down at #2. Working from right to left, bring needle up at odd numbers and take it down at even numbers. The center stitch (5 to 6) is worked in red or green yarn and can be skipped over now and filled in later. For the second row, bring needle up one hole below #3 and take it down at #1. Still working from right to left, make two more stitches beside this one.

By this time you should be able to follow the Noel Chart, taking one stitch for each symbol on the chart. The symbol " Δ " is for white stitches; the symbol " ● " is for red or green stitches. When working on green canvas, work these stitches in red; when working on red canvas, work these stitches in green.

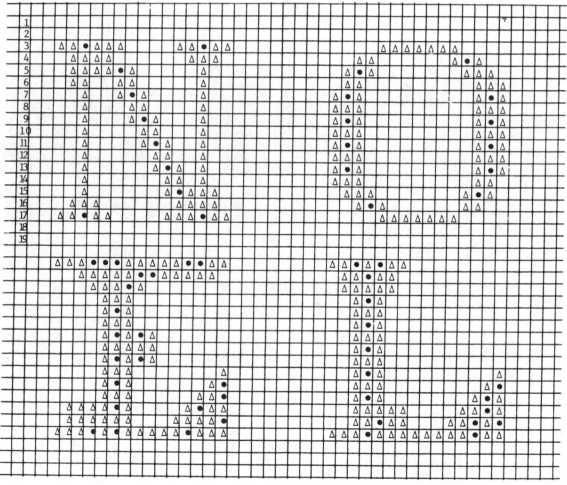

Noel Chart

Snowman Decoration

Hold plastic canvas sheet so that the longer edges are at the top and bottom and the shorter edges are at the sides. Next, count in to the 33rd hole from either left or right edge. Cut from top to bottom along this vertical row of holes. Cut another piece the same size. This decoration is worked in cross-stitch throughout. See Figure B for cross-stitch directions.

To start the letter "J," count in 17 holes from left edge and seven holes down from top. Bring needle up in this hole to make first cross-stitch. Make two more cross-stitches to the right of the first one. You now have the top bar of the letter "J." Now follow chart at left, making one cross-stitch for each symbol on chart. Use white yarn wherever the symbol " Δ " appears. Use red, black, or green for all other symbols. Where three blank squares appear between letters and between last letter and snowman, skip three canvas threads (which will be two holes skipped).

Work the same design on each of the two pieces of canvas. Work one crocheted chain approximately 17 inches long for top and another approximately 7 inches long for bottom. Leave a 3-inch or 4-inch length of yarn at each end of each chain. Thread one end of yarn into tapestry needle and take two or three stitches through a corner hole of one of the canvas pieces. Do the same in each of the other corners, thus securing the long chain to top and the shorter chain to bottom. About 1½ inches down from top of top chain make an overhand knot. Cut 16 strands of yarn, each 8 inches long. Holding all strands together, lay them over the lower chain having all ends together. With a 5-inch strand of yarn, wrap twice around tassel, about ½ inch from top and tie in knot.

 Figure B

Snowman Chart

137

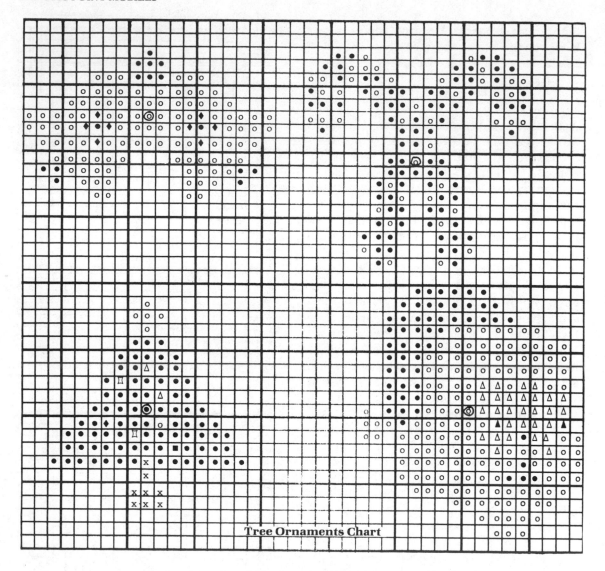

Tree Ornaments Chart

Tree Ornaments

There are four optional ornament designs charted above. In top left corner you will see two bells. Below bells is a Christmas tree. In top right corner are two candy canes and below that is a Santa face. The tree and candy canes can be worked on squares same size as Noel mobile squares. For the other two, cut each square two holes wider in each direction. Center stitch is circled in each design.

Colors: Work Santa and candy canes on green canvas, using white for each "o" and red for each " ● "; for Santa, use black yarn for " ▲ ." Work bell and tree on red canvas, using green for each " ● " and white for each "o." Work each " ♦ " on bell in red. All other symbols on tree are to be worked in color of your choice.

BRIDGE COASTERS

MATERIALS

One 10½-by-13-inch sheet of 10-mesh plastic canvas (will make at least eight coasters)

Acrylic yarn in either 4-ply knitting worsted-weight or Persian-type needlepoint yarn. For a set of four coasters, you will need approximately:

    72 yards white
    15 yards red
    15 yards black

#18 tapestry needle

For the coasters, you should cut four squares, with each square having 32 holes in each direction. After cutting the squares, trim all sides so that there are no "nubby" edges. No further finishing is needed.

Regular canvas made from natural fibers could be used for the coasters but would not have the body or stiffness of those made with the plastic canvas. Also, they would not wash as well. If you use the recommended plastic canvas and acrylic yarns, the coasters can even

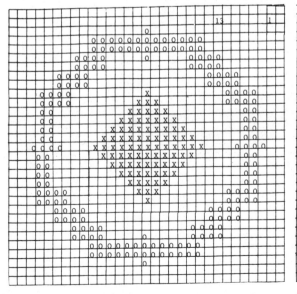

Color Code: X = red   O = black   ☐ = white

be washed in the washing machine. Do not put them in an electric or gas dryer, however. Just lay them flat on any smooth surface to dry.

You will find, with the plastic canvas, that it is easier to work bringing the needle up through the canvas in one motion and taking it down in another motion instead of going into one hole and out another in a single motion as you may be accustomed to doing.

MERRY CHRISTMAS ORNAMENTS

MATERIALS

Two 10½-by-13-inch sheets of 10-mesh plastic canvas

Approximately 80 yards each of red, green, and white yarn and 2 yards of gold yarn—Persian-type needlepoint yarn is recommended

STITCH AND COLOR KEY

Design #1: Design in center of photo is stitched in red and white (light lines are white, heavy lines are red, Smyrna stitch in center is red). Smyrna stitches around outer edge are green. Background Gobelin stitches are white. A Gobelin stitch is simply a long, straight stitch made over the number of canvas threads as designated by lines on the chart.

Design #2: First work one Rhodes stitch in center using red yarn; work a row of three-thread Scotch stitches with green yarn around all sides of the Rhodes stitch. Follow with four rows of Smyrna stitches in the following color sequence: red, white, red, green.

Design #3: Light center lines are yellow Gobelin stitches; heavy center lines are red. Light outer lines are white; heavy outer lines are green.

Design #4: Entire design is worked in tent stitch (also known as continental, half-cross, or basketweave). Bells and lettering are red. Top of bell and clappers are green (x). Background is white with final outside row stitched in green.

Design #5: Heavy lines in center are four leaf stitch patterns. Work them in red with a yellow center and green foliage. For rice stitch around the outer edge, work red crosses with green crossed corners. Background is white.

Design #6: Tree and border are green; background is white. Tent stitch is used for tree and background; border is Scotch stitch.

Design #7: Eight-pointed star (heavy center lines) is red with a white cross-stitch in center. Light center lines are white. Three rows of tent stitch frame the center design (heavy lines are green, light lines are white). The Scotch-stitch border is green.

Design #8: Long and short slanting stitches form a pattern known as Milanese stitch.

141

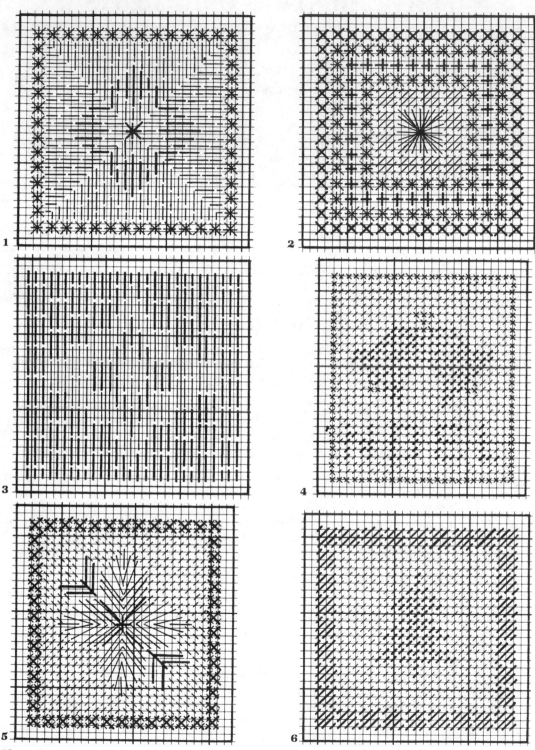

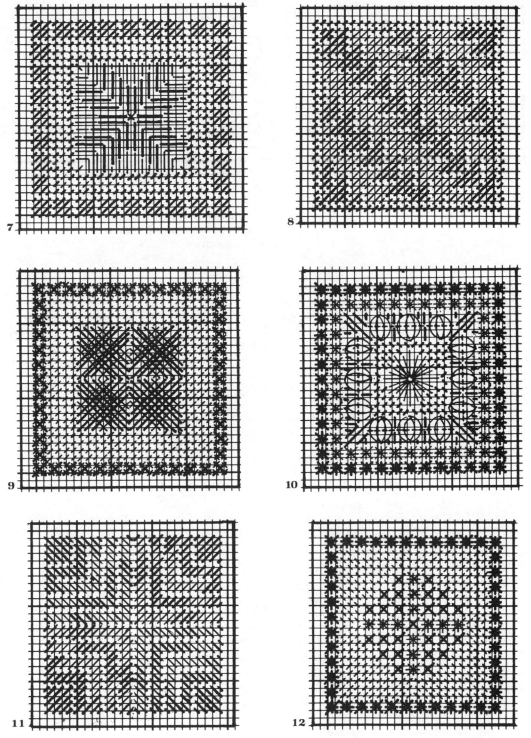

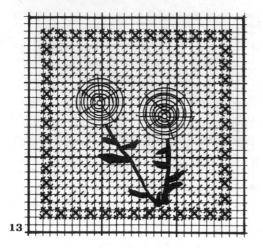

13

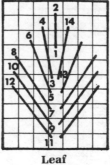

Leaf

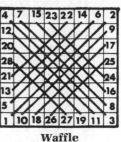

Waffle

Note: Bring needle up at odd numbers; take needle down at even numbers.

Scotch Stitch

Smyrna

Rice

Rococo

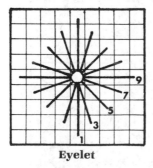

Eyelet

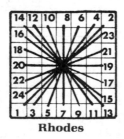

Rhodes

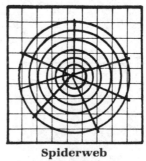

Spiderweb (7-spoke)

Heavy lines are green, light lines are white. Start in upper left-hand corner and work diagonally to lower right corner with green, making the stitches the length shown on the chart.

Design #9: (not shown in photograph) Work four seven-thread waffle stitches in center in red; work a border of rice stitch around outside edges, using red for cross-stitch and green to cross the corners; fill in remaining space with tent stitches.

Design #10: Center eyelet is white, surrounded by a square of red tent stitches. Rococo stitches are white against a background of green. Border is two rows of Smyrna stitches (light for red, heavy for green). This design may be a bit too complex for the beginner.

Design #11: Center star is white (light lines). Work first pattern of heavy lines in red to form second star outline. Work second pattern of light lines in white to form outer star. Background (outer heavy lines) is green.

Design #12: Center design is worked in red and white Smyrna stitches (light are white, heavy are red). The border is made of green Smyrna stitches, background is white tent stitches, slanted as shown in the diagram.

Design #13: The roses are made of red "spiderweb" stitches. First work any odd number of spokes (the long, slanting stitches shown on our seven-spoke diagram). Then, weave the yarn alternately under and over the spokes until you think they can hold no more, then add at least one more row. Rice stitch border is worked with red crosses and green crossed corners. Embroider the leaves and stems in green when balance of design is complete. Advanced design.

Note: Full three-ply strands are used for all stitches except Smyrna, which uses only two strands.

Counted Cross-Stitch

When you hear the word "cross-stitch," does it bring to mind dishtowels and pillowcases in inexpensive fabric stamped with large Xs for you to cover with embroidery threads?

I must confess that this was my conception—and it really turned me off—until I visited Denmark in 1970 and for the first time saw beautiful examples of counted cross-stitch worked on even-weave fabrics.

Whenever I travel, I always seek out needlework shops and, on my first day in Copenhagen, I found a charming shop with a window full of what I thought was exquisitely fine needlepoint.

When I entered the shop, however, and examined the work closely, I could see that the designs were worked on fabric instead of canvas, with the fabric itself serving as background.

On the spot, I purchased fabrics, charts, and embroidery floss. Since counted cross-stitch goes so quickly, I had finished all of the projects soon after my return home. To my dismay, it was almost impossible to find the fabrics in needlework shops in my area or by mail order.

At that time, our country was sadly behind the rest of the world as far as counted-thread embroidery of any type was concerned. Although it is often called Danish cross-stitch, this type of needlework is part of the culture of all European countries and many Asian, African, Central and South American nations as well.

Fortunately, times have changed and many specialty shops carry the linen, Aida, and Hardanger cloth so well suited to this type of stitchery.

These are fabrics in which the horizontal and vertical threads are woven the same distance apart, thus permitting a perfectly square stitch to be achieved when working over thread intersections.

If you can thread a needle and go up in one hole and down in another, you can do counted cross-stitch. It is fortunate that this is an inexpensive form of needlecraft, for you are likely to become addicted to it and there is no end to the items you can adorn with cross-stitch. One reader told me, "Pat, you're not just a cross-stitch addict—you're a pusher!"

The count of a cross-stitch fabric indicates the number of stitches per inch that will result when working over one intersection of threads. A 14-count fabric, for instance, will result in 14 stitches per inch.

In some very finely woven fabrics, you will be told to work over two or more threads with each stitch, resulting in a lower stitch count. Two examples of this are the Gothic Alphabet Pillows on p. 153 and the Steeplechase Picture on p. 161.

The better known cross-stitch fabrics are Aida, Hardanger, and linen, but any fine quality even-weave fabric can be used and we are now seeing a wider variety come into use in this country as the popularity of counted work explodes. Some of the other fabrics coming into more widespread use are Davos, Gerta, Floba, Dublin, Klosters, and Fiddler's Cloth, to name a few.

Embroidery floss is generally packaged in skeins of six-strand floss. How many of these six strands to use at a time is a matter of choice and can best be determined by experimenting. As a general rule, however, you will use just one strand on any fabric with a thread count of 22 or higher (when you are working over just one fabric thread), two strands for 14- and 18-count fabric, and three strands for 11-count Aida. Persian-type tapestry yarns are good choices for fabrics with loose weaves.

If you are a needlepointer, you may feel that you need more strands to cover the fabric—but that's not really the idea with counted cross-stitch. Traditionally, it has a light, airy look to it that is lost when you overpower it with several strands used in the needle.

Fabric Preparation Before you take the first stitch you need to prepare the fabric so that it will not ravel. You can turn under and stitch a small hem, work a row of zigzag stitches on your sewing machine, or you can overcast the edges. If this seems like a lot of bother to you, you can resort to the use of masking tape to bind the edges, but I personally feel that it is better to hem the edges. Be sure to allow a little excess margin for turning under when framing or finishing your pieces.

These subjects are covered in the section on working from graph charts. I suggest that you now turn to p. 9-12 for this information.

Design Size and Placement

Threads are secured in much the same manner as in needle-point, running the needle through a few previously worked stitches when you start a new strand or finish an old one. See the information on the waste-knot technique on p. 6. The use of a knot, even in this temporary fashion, is frowned upon by many purists, but I still find it the easiest way to start.

To Begin Stitching

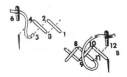

Illustration #1

The accepted method of starting the first stitch in a previously unworked area is to hold the beginning thread below the fabric until it is secured by the first few stitches. Try both methods and choose the one that suits you best.

You can work the cross-stitches singly or in horizontal or vertical rows. The one unbreakable rule is that you should always cross all stitches in one direction.

To work a row of cross-stitch, following Illustration #1, bring the needle up from wrong to right side at odd numbers and take the needle down from right to wrong side at even numbers, following the numerical sequence given for a row of three cross-stitches. The first part of the chart shows you how to work the base stitch (1 through 6) and the second part shows you how to complete the cross-stitch (7 through 12). You will notice that the base stitches slant from right to left.

Illustration #2

Illustration #2 shows you how to work with the base stitch slanting from left to right. Either method is correct, but, on any single piece, select one or the other so that all stitches are crossed in the same direction.

Illustration #3 shows you the way to work vertical rows. Again, be sure to cross all stitches in the same direction. Illustrations #2 and #3 show the cross-stitches worked over single threads and over double threads.

While counted-thread embroidery encompasses most embroidery stitches, as a general rule, counted cross-stitch usually consists of only the cross-stitch and the back stitch (also known as straight stitch).

Illustration #3

The back stitch is often used to define design outlines or as an accent. It is a single stitch, worked horizontally, vertically, or slanted. See Illustration #4.

Always secure and snip off threads as you go. Loose ends dangling on the wrong side are sure to become tangled and knotty, showing as unsightly lumps on the right side of your work.

It is usually best to work small areas at a time, securing the

Illustration #4

final loose thread end before moving on to the next area. It might not be noticeable at the time, but threads extending across the back of the piece over unworked areas will often show up as shadows on the finished piece, so do avoid this.

Most people prefer working with an embroidery hoop, keeping the fabric fairly taut as you work. Some experienced stitchers can do beautiful work holding the fabric over the index finger of the left hand, but I don't really recommend this for the average cross-stitcher.

One of the first reactions for many who have never done this type of work is: "Oh, I could never do that—the holes are too small, and I would strain my eyes doing that."

Please don't let that deter you unless you have a severe vision problem. Even then, there are large magnifying glasses designed to be worn around the neck, so that you can look through them and still have your hands free to work.

Also, you will be surprised to learn that you really don't have to clearly "see" the holes—your needle will search them out. As you are working, you can develop the habit of letting the point of the needle slide across the work, seeking out the holes in the fabric. Even though the fabric surface looks smooth, try running the point over the fabric and see how it feels slightly bumpy as you do so.

If your fingers are relaxed, you will see how the needle does seek out the openings in the fabric. When you think about it, that's what you do to bring the needle up from the wrong side. If you did not, you would be constantly turning the hoop over for each stitch, so isn't it logical to let your needle find the place on the right side as well?

Counted Cross-Stitch Projects

GOTHIC ALPHABET PILLOWS

MATERIALS

22-to-the-inch Hardanger fabric or 21-to-the-inch evenweave fabric
J. & P. Coats deluxe 6-strand floss
Backing fabric for each pillow
Foam or cotton stuffing OR pillow forms to fit

Pillow A: (Letter A in photo)
Cut fabric square 17-by-17 inches
five skeins #120 crimson
two skeins #224 nectarine
finished size: 16-by-16 inches

Pillow B: (Letter S in photo)
Cut fabric piece 21-by-15 inches
five skeins #28-b treeleaf green
two skeins #5-A chartreuse
finished size: 20-by-14 inches

Pillow C: (Letters MG in photo)
Cut fabric piece 21-by-15 inches
five skeins #81-B dark colonial brown
two skeins #213 beige
finished size: 20-by-14 inches

Embroidery: Use four strands of 6-strand floss throughout. Diagram 1 consists of the complete alphabet. The main color is worked within the outlined areas, omitting any small areas marked with a cross. The second color is worked within the solid areas. Diagrams 2 and 3 give a section of the repetitive design for each border with small dots representing the main color and solid areas the second color. Each square of the chart represents one cross-stitch taken over three threads of fabric.

Centering Design: Fold fabric piece in half vertically and run a basting thread along fold to mark vertical center; fold in half in other direction and run basting thread along fold to mark horizontal center. Exact center is point where basting threads cross. For Pillows A or B, find center of chosen letter and have the center stitch in center of fabric. For Pillow C, it is best to chart the two chosen initials on a piece of graph paper. As letters vary in width, the center will depend upon your choice. After charting your choice of letters, fold graph in half both ways to determine center.

Finishing: Press on wrong side on a padded surface. Cut backing piece to same measurements. With wrong sides together, machine-stitch the two pieces together around three sides leaving a ½-inch seam allowance on each side. Turn to right side and press all edges, turning under ½-inch hem on open edges. Insert pillow form and sew remaining edge by hand.

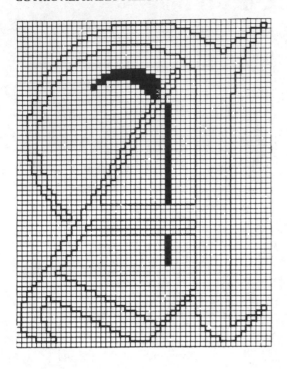

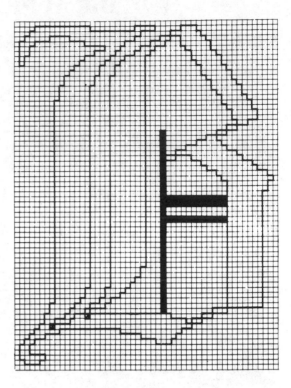

Diagram 1

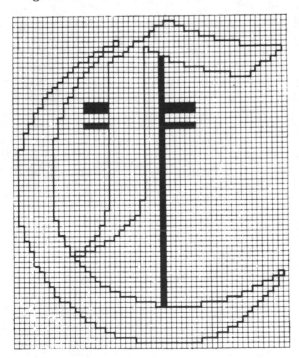

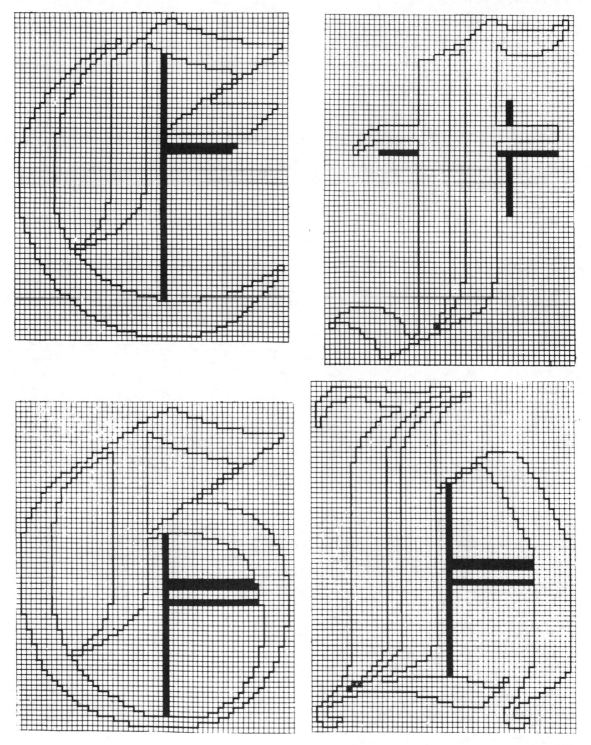

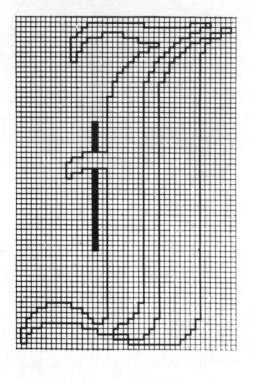

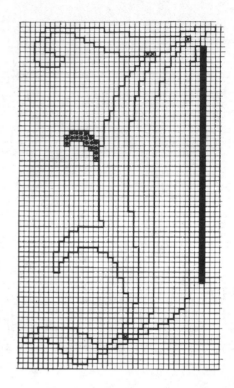

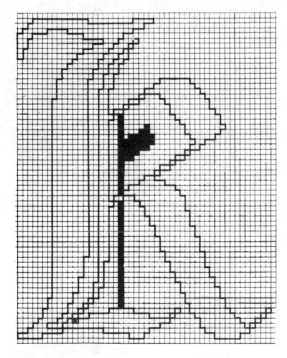

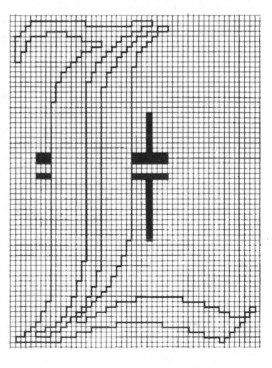

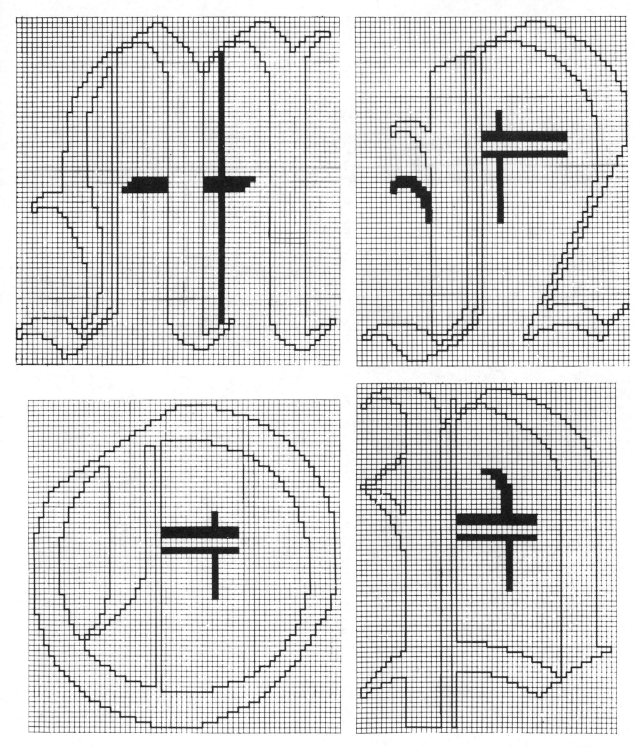

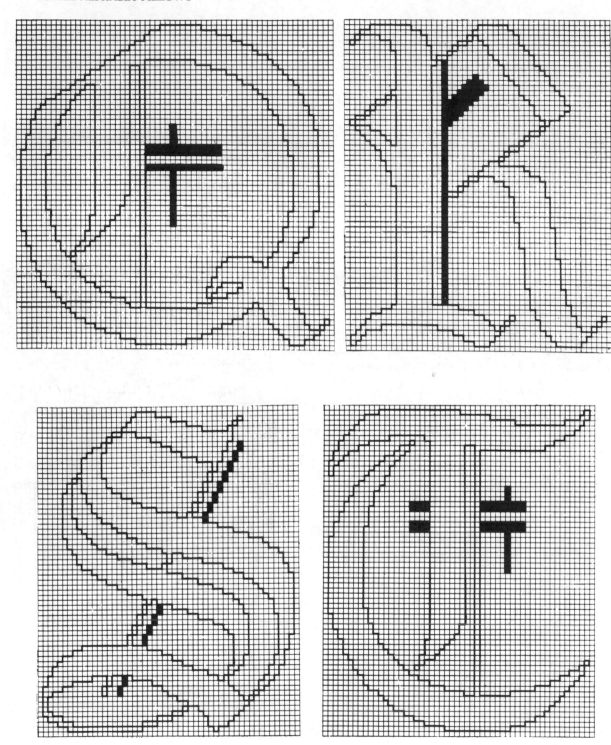

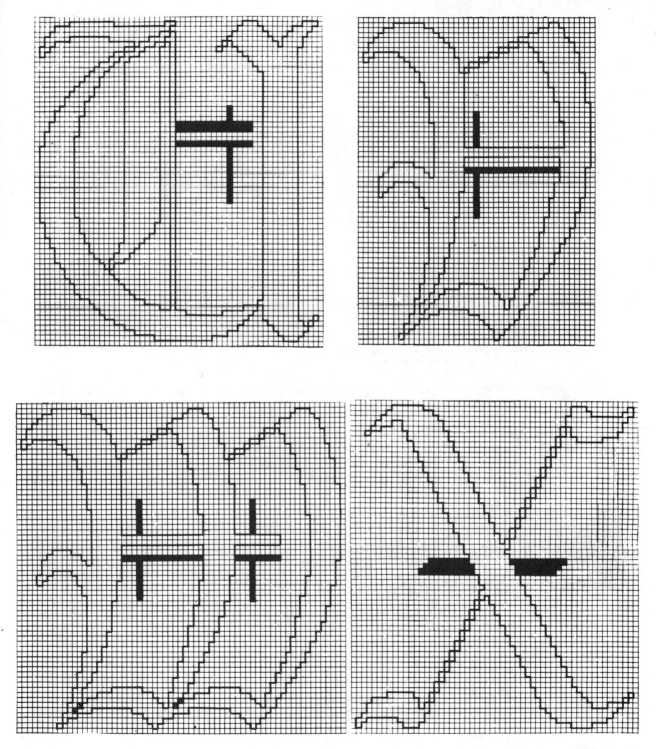

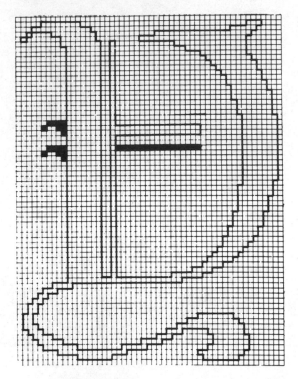

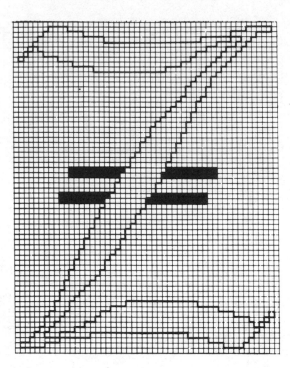

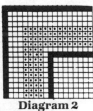

Diagram 2

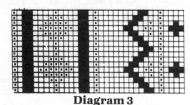

Diagram 3

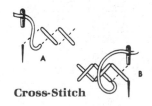

Cross-Stitch

Remember: Each strand of floss is made up of six separate strands. Separate strands and thread needle with four strands.

Getting Started: Once—and once only—you will make a knot in the floss threaded in your needle. Pass the needle through from right to wrong side of fabric about 2 inches to the left of point where first stitch will be taken having the knot on the right side of fabric. As you work your first row of stitches, the strand will lay across the back of your work and will be covered with stitches, thus securing it. When you come close to the knot, snip it off. Make no more knots. Instead, secure beginning and ending threads by running through the back of previously worked stitches. To avoid tangles, always snip loose ends as soon as you have secured them.

Cross-Stitch: Bring needle through from wrong to right side at point where first stitch is to be made. *Count across three threads diagonally and take needle down.* Next bring needle up three threads directly below the point where you last took needle down and repeat from *to* (Figure A). Continue to end of row in this manner. On the return journey, complete the other half of the cross (Figure B). It is important that the top strands of all the stitches point in one direction.

STEEPLECHASE PICTURE

MATERIALS

One 20-by-22-inch piece of evenweave fabric with 22 threads to the inch

#24 tapestry needle

J. & P. Coats deluxe 6-strand embroidery floss; one skein of each of following colors:

#124	Indian pink
#218	coral glow
#140	signal red
#51C	gold brown
#62	russet
#70	silver gray
#213	beige
#71	pewter gray
# 1	white
#12	black
#211	charcoal*

*#211 charcoal has recently been discontinued. If you are unable to find this color, you may substitute DMC Color #645.

For ease in identifying the colors and keeping them separate, punch 11 holes in a piece of cardboard. Label each hole with a color number. Slip the label from a skein and cut the threads in 18-inch lengths. Loop the threads through the hole and secure with a loose loop knot.

Preparing the Fabric: To prevent raveling, turn under a small hem all around and stitch in place by hand or machine or stitch around all edges with a double row of zigzag stitches. Fold the fabric in half from top to bottom and run a line of basting thread along the fold line; then fold fabric in half from side to side and run a line of basting thread along this fold. Where the basting threads cross is the center of your fabric.

Following the Chart: The arrows on the chart point to the horizontal and vertical centers of the design. Fold the chart along the row pointed to by the arrow on the right edge. This will give you the horizontal center. Make another fold in the chart along the row shown by the lower arrow, giving you the vertical center.

Each symbol on the chart represents one cross-stitch. You may start in the center of the design and work out in all directions, but I recommend that you start at the center top of the design with the top row of stitches for the rider's hat. Follow the vertical basting line up to a point 6 inches above the horizontal basting line and take the first stitch there. After working the first horizontal row of the hat, work the row just below it. If you will continue in this manner, working across and down, you will find it relatively easy to follow the chart.

Each strand of embroidery floss is made up of six strands. Separate the strands before threading the needle and use only three strands in the needle. With first strands, make a knot in the long end and pass needle through from right to wrong side of fabric about 2 inches to the right of the point where first stitch will be made, having the knot on the right side of the fabric. As you work the first row of stitches, the strand will lay across the back of your work and will be covered with the stitches, thus securing it. Later you will snip away the knot. From this point on, make no more knots. Secure thread ends by running them through the back of stitches already worked. To avoid tangles, always snip loose ends of threads as soon as you have secured them.

Finishing: When embroidery is completed, press embroidery on wrong side. Select a frame of suitable size. Cut a piece of fiber board or heavy cardboard just slightly smaller than frame. Center the embroidery on the backing board and secure with pins into edge of board. Secure at back by lacing both ways with a strong thread. Remove pins and place in frame.

Remember: Fabric has 22 threads per inch. Work over two threads for each stitch giving you a gauge of 11 stitches per inch.

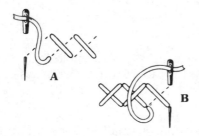

Color Code

[L] —	70	silver gray
✕ —	213	beige
▨ —	71	pewter gray
◪ —	211	charcoal
✛ —	218	coral glow
Z —	140	signal red
● —	12	black
· —	1	white
⊟ —	124	Indian pink
⊟ —	62	russet
⊘ —	51C	gold brown

Cross-Stitch: Bring the needle through on the lower right line of the cross and insert at the top of the same line, taking a stitch through the fabric to lower left line (A). Continue to the end of the row in this way; on the return journey, complete the other half of the cross (B). It is important that the top strands of all the stitches point in one direction.

Designs in cross-stitch should be worked over counted threads of canvas or evenweave fabric to have the best result.

CHRISTMAS ORNAMENTS

MATERIALS

One 6-by-12-inch piece 18-count Aida cloth

Six 2¼-inch round frames

6-strand embroidery floss in following colors:
 bright red
 medium red
 emerald green
 medium blue
 medium pink
 pale pink
 yellow
 deep gold
 brown
 black

#22-24 needle

small embroidery hoop

Note: Always thread needle with just two of the six strands. One skein in each of the colors will be more than sufficient.

Preparation: To prevent raveling of the fabric, you should whip-stitch, hem, or zigzag-stitch the edges.

 With a basting thread, mark the fabric into six 3-inch squares.

 To be sure that your design is centered, it is suggested that you start by working the center stitch first and then working down from that point. When the lower half of the design is complete, turn chart and embroidery upside down and work in the opposite direction. The center lines of each chart are marked by arrows. To find the center of your fabric, fold one 3-inch section in half both vertically and horizontally; the center stitch of the design should fall where the creases in the fabric meet. Begin with the stitch nearest this point.

 Each symbol on the charts represents one stitch; the color code shows you which color to use for each symbol. All stitches are worked in cross-stitch except for those marked with a slash (/) or dashes(--). Where these appear, work in backstitch.

Finishing: Place embroidery face down on a folded towel or similar padded surface and press with a warm iron. Gradually increase temperature of iron if piece is not completely smooth. If your frame does not have a cardboard backing, cut a circle of cardboard to fit in frame. Cut embroidered fabric in a circle just barely larger than the backing. Using white glue, such as Sobo glue, glue the fabric to the cardboard back and insert in frame.

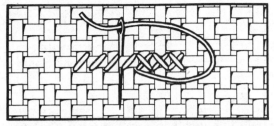

Do all the stitches in the same color in the same row, working left to right and slanting from bottom left to upper right. Then cross back, completing the Xs.

Some cross-stitchers prefer to cross each stitch as they come to it; this is fine, but be sure the slant is always in the correct direction.

Of course, isolated stitches must be crossed as you work them. Vertical stitches are crossed as shown.

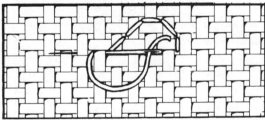

The only other stitch used in counted cross-stitch is the backstitch. This is worked from hole to hole and may be vertical, horizontal, or slanted.

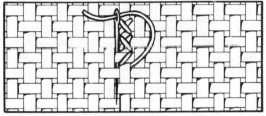

When carrying a color from one area to another, wiggle your needle under existing stitches on the underside. Do not carry a color across an open expanse of fabric for more than a few stitches as the thread will be visible from the front.

To end a color, weave in and out of the underside of stitches, perhaps making a scallop stitch or two for extra security.

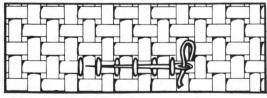

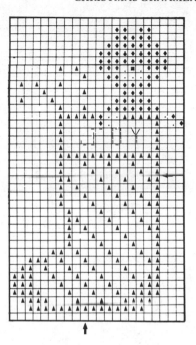

Color Code:

● — emerald green

▲ — bright red

△ — medium red

X — medium blue

⋈ — pink

  — pale pink

o — yellow

◆ — deep gold

■ — brown

◗ — black

/ — This mark, turned in either direction, is to be worked in half a cross-stitch. On the snowman, work it in red. On the sled, work it in brown.

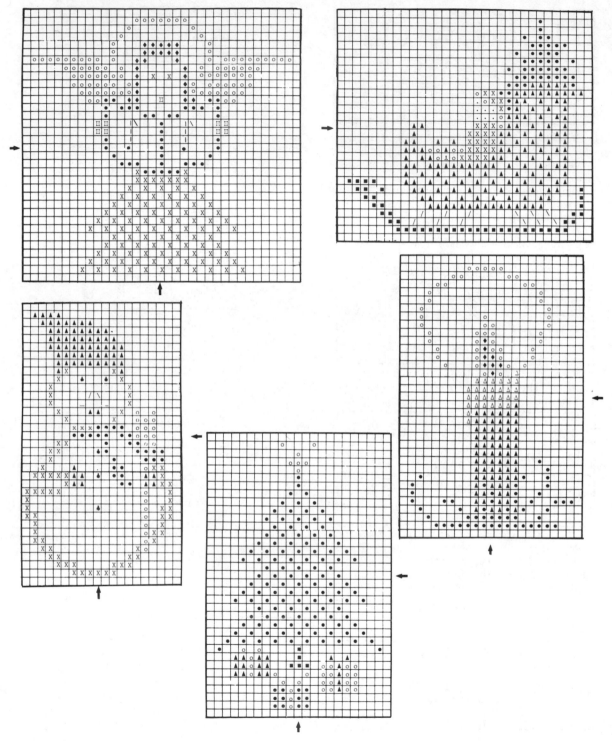

ALICE IN WONDERLAND
BIRTH SAMPLER PILLOW

MATERIALS

11-, 14-, or 18-count Aida—one inch larger in each direction than desired finished size of pillow

Finished Design Area Measurements on Various Aida Fabrics:

11-count Aida = 6-by-7½ inches
14-count Aida = 4¾-by-6 inches
18-count Aida = 3¾-by-4⅔ inches

(These measurements are approximate and are for the area filled with stitches only. Additional space must be allowed around all sides of the design area.)

One skein DMC floss in each color listed in Color Code:

X 642 beige
≡ 842 light tan
O 955 light aqua
● 993 medium aqua
X 943 dark aqua
· 776 light pink
    956 dark pink (eye, nose)
N 3042 very light gray
Z 318 medium gray
▲ 309 dark rose
Z silver metallic
╪ 415 light gray

Design by Ginnie Thompson Originals, Inc.

Use alphabet and graph space below to graph name & date.
Count stitches and center on arrow below rabbit.

KEY HANG-UPS

MATERIALS

18-count Aida cloth, 4-by-8 inches

One skein DMC floss for each color listed in color code

3-to-3½-inch gold frame with glass

Design by

Ginnie Thompson Originals, Inc.

Instructions: Prepare the fabric by whipping, hemming, or zigzagging on the sewing machine at the edges to prevent fraying. Find the center of the design; fold your fabric to find its center. Count from the center of the design to where you wish to begin; we recommend the top of the design as a good starting place. Count corresponding squares of your fabric to this starting point. Use two threads in your needle for Aida and linen or to stitch over two squares each way on Hardanger. Use one strand in your needle for going over one square of Hardanger.

Thread should be cut to approximately 18 inches. Or, if two strands are used, cut the thread to 36 inches and double each strand.

(Optional) Place the area to be worked in a hoop. Keep the fabric taut and the holes will be easy to find.

Don't use knots; begin the thread by catching the end under the first few stitches on the back. End by wiggling the thread through existing stitches on the back.

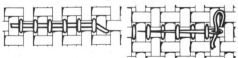

Tension: Be firm but gentle. The stitches should be flat with no distortion of the fabric.

Washing Instructions: Wash in cold water with mild soap. Roll the washed piece in a towel and squeeze out the moisture. Then iron it under a protective covering such as a handkerchief or linen towel.

Mounting: Disassemble the frames, being careful to put the small hooks in a safe place. Lay glass over your sampler and cut the fabric carefully with sharp scissors to the exact size of the glass. Reassemble—glass first, then cross-stitch, then hook, then backing.

DMC colors:

726 yellow

434 brown

336 dark blue, *backstitch hood ornament*

321 red

904 green, *backstitch flower stem*

413 dark gray, *backstitch cat, car lights*

356 rust, *backstitch doormat, steps, bricks*

415 gray, *backstitch car radiator*

312 blue, *backstitch door*

334 light blue, *backstitch car top*

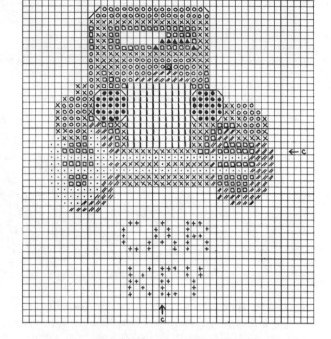

Cross-Stitch

Always make the top stitch in the same direction. When possible, do a row of understitches, then cross back. Do not carry a thread across more than five spaces. It will show through.

Variations are as illustrated.

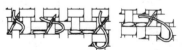

Backstitch

Backstitches can go in any direction. They are indicated on the graph by straight lines. When the graph indicates a straight line covering more than one square, stitch one backstitch per square rather than one long stitch. Long stitches disrupt the texture of the finished piece.

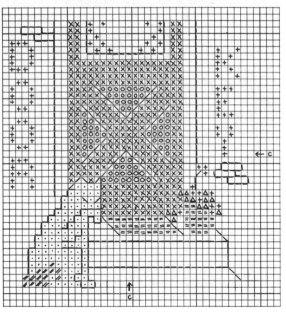

170

PICNIC MENU

MATERIALS

14-count Aida, 30-by-12 inches (finished size = 28-by-9¼ inches) OR
18-count Aida, 24-by-10 inches (finished size = 21⅔-by-7¼ inches)
One skein DMC floss in each color listed except #310 black and #326 red
for which you will need two skeins

Image size: 390 stitches wide by 128 stitches high

Design by Ginnie Thompson Originals, Inc.

Color Code:

DMC Art. 117

310 black ●	895 dark green Z
326 red Λ	677 cream ·
838 dark brown ▲	841 tan S
436 gold brown O	839 dark tan +
796 royal blue X	738 light gold C
518 bright blue V	
3325 light blue L	
986 medium green I	
471 light green —	
947 orange H	

Backstitch around stump in dark tan **1**

Backstitch in medium green **2**

Backstitch ant legs and antenna in same color as body **3**

Do back stitching last so it won't be obscured by later stitches.

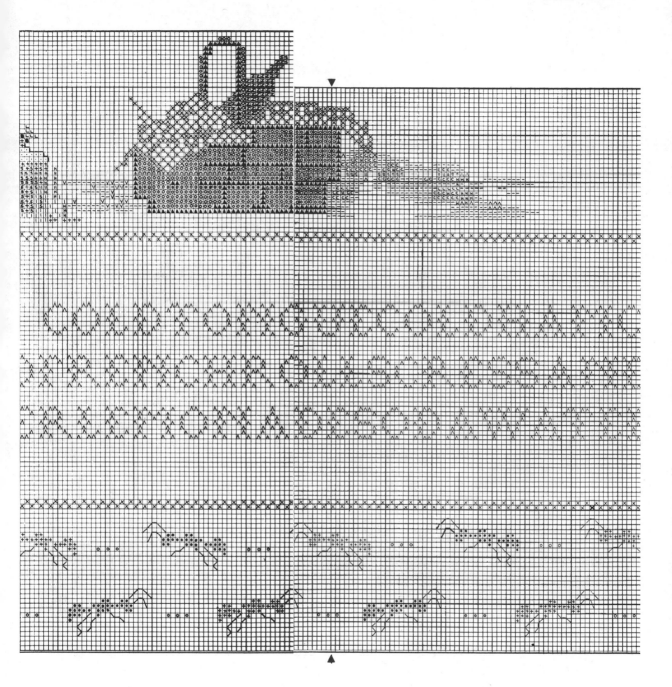

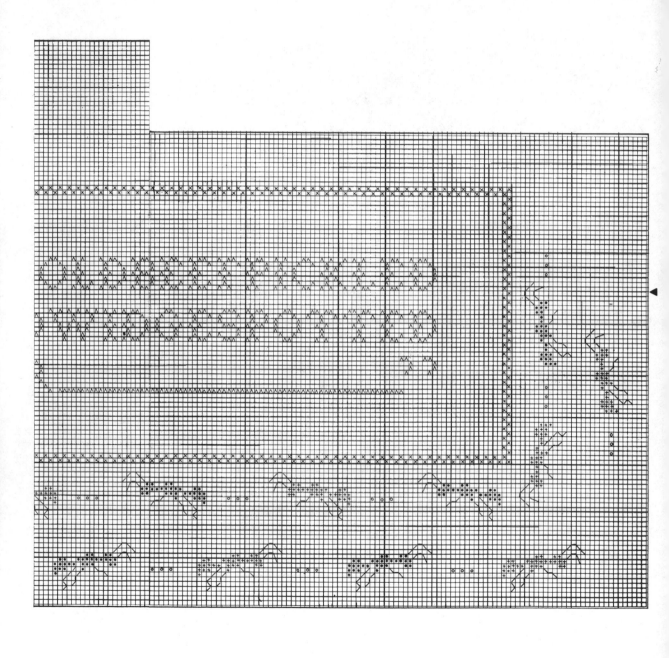

Stitchery Sayings

The charts on the pages that follow have been designed to use for needlepoint. To use them for counted cross-stitch, make one full cross-stitch wherever a line or symbol crosses a grid of the chart. Some of the following instructions are related to needlepoint, but most can be adapted to cross-stitch.

Selection of Materials

Any size of canvas or fabric can be used. The size you select will determine the finished size of your piece. Mesh count or thread count is based on the number of single stitches that can be made over 1 inch of canvas or fabric. For example, on a 14-mesh or a 14-count fabric, you would get 14 stitches per inch.

Refer to the needlepoint and cross-stitch chapters for information on yarns and floss.

Finished Sizes

To determine the finished size of your piece, divide the stitch counts by the mesh count of your canvas or the thread count of your fabric. In other words, if the horizontal stitch count is 140 and you have a 14-mesh or thread count, your finished piece would be 10 inches wide. With 10-count materials, the finished piece would be 14 inches wide.

Borders

On the charts where borders are shown, the borders are included in the stitch counts. If no border is shown, you will have to allow extra canvas and fabric for the border. You may design your own, use one from one of the other charts, or select one from the chart on p. 178.

Here are some tips for figuring how much extra material you will need for any of these borders. Borders 2, 3, and 4 are very simple to plan. Just count the meshes or threads covered horizontally and vertically and allow a multiple of these numbers. For example, Border No. 3 covers four threads in each direction. Thus, with 12-mesh canvas, you would need one-third of an inch additional on all sides plus at least that much for spacing above, below, and at side edges of central design. These three are designed for needlepoint rather than cross-stitch.

More elaborate borders require more planning. Border No. 5 covers five threads in each direction for each corner and four threads are needed for every repeat.

Border No. 1 must be very carefully planned. If you use this or any other border requiring a large number of stitches for corners and repeats, it is wise to work your border first and then center the design within the border. Better yet, pencil in the border stitches on your design chart, starting at centers and working out. I suggest a pencil rather than a pen as you are likely to be erasing at some points.

In Border No. 1, the corner stitches include all of those from one arrow to the last stitch in the corner in each direction. You will need 30 meshes or threads in each direction to work each corner of this design. Each full design repeat between corners requires 37 threads. Therefore, if you plan one center design repeat, you will cover 97 threads (30 for each corner and 37 for the repeat). Two design repeats would cover 134 threads and three design repeats would cover 171 threads. So, on 12-mesh canvas, one side from corner to corner would cover $8\frac{1}{12}$ inches for a single repeat, $11\frac{1}{6}$ inches for two repeats, and $14\frac{1}{4}$ inches for three repeats. All of the examples are for 12-mesh canvas but use the same principles for figuring requirements for any size of canvas or fabric.

Canvas or Fabric Requirements

For needlepoint, be sure to allow an additional 2 inches of unworked canvas for all edges, and for cross-stitch be sure to allow an additional inch of fabric beyond that needed for design and border on all edges. To be sure, unless you are experienced at figuring material requirements, it is wise to purchase canvas or fabric at least 3 or 4 inches wider and deeper than you think necessary. The cost of a few extra inches of either is minor when you consider it a guarantee that your project will be completed satisfactorily.

Starting a Design

If you want to start at one edge of the canvas or fabric, you must carefully count the squares of the graph horizontally and vertically and do the same with the holes of the canvas to be sure that the design is centered properly. As this can be tedious, most people prefer to find the center of the chart and the center of the canvas or fabric and begin there—working out in all directions from the center. See directions for centering in needlepoint chapter (p. 10).

The Bargello border used for the third stitchery saying chart that follows (Kindness Is the Golden Chain . . .) was adapted from the book, *Bargello Borders*, by Jean Riley and Nancy Hall (previously mentioned in traditional canvas section). This is an exceptionally good book for needlepointers and, if not available in your favorite needlepoint shop, can be ordered by mail. To obtain a copy, send a check or money order for $11.95 plus $2 for postage and handling to: Needlemania, Inc., P.O. Box 123, Franklin, Michigan 48025.

Borders Chart

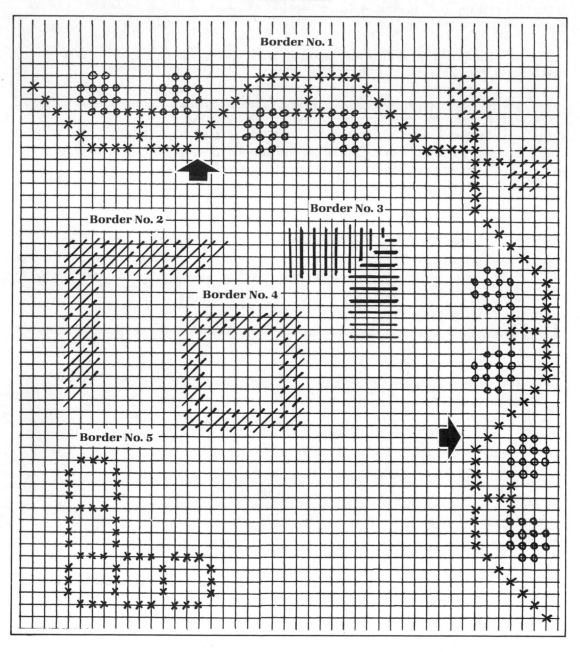

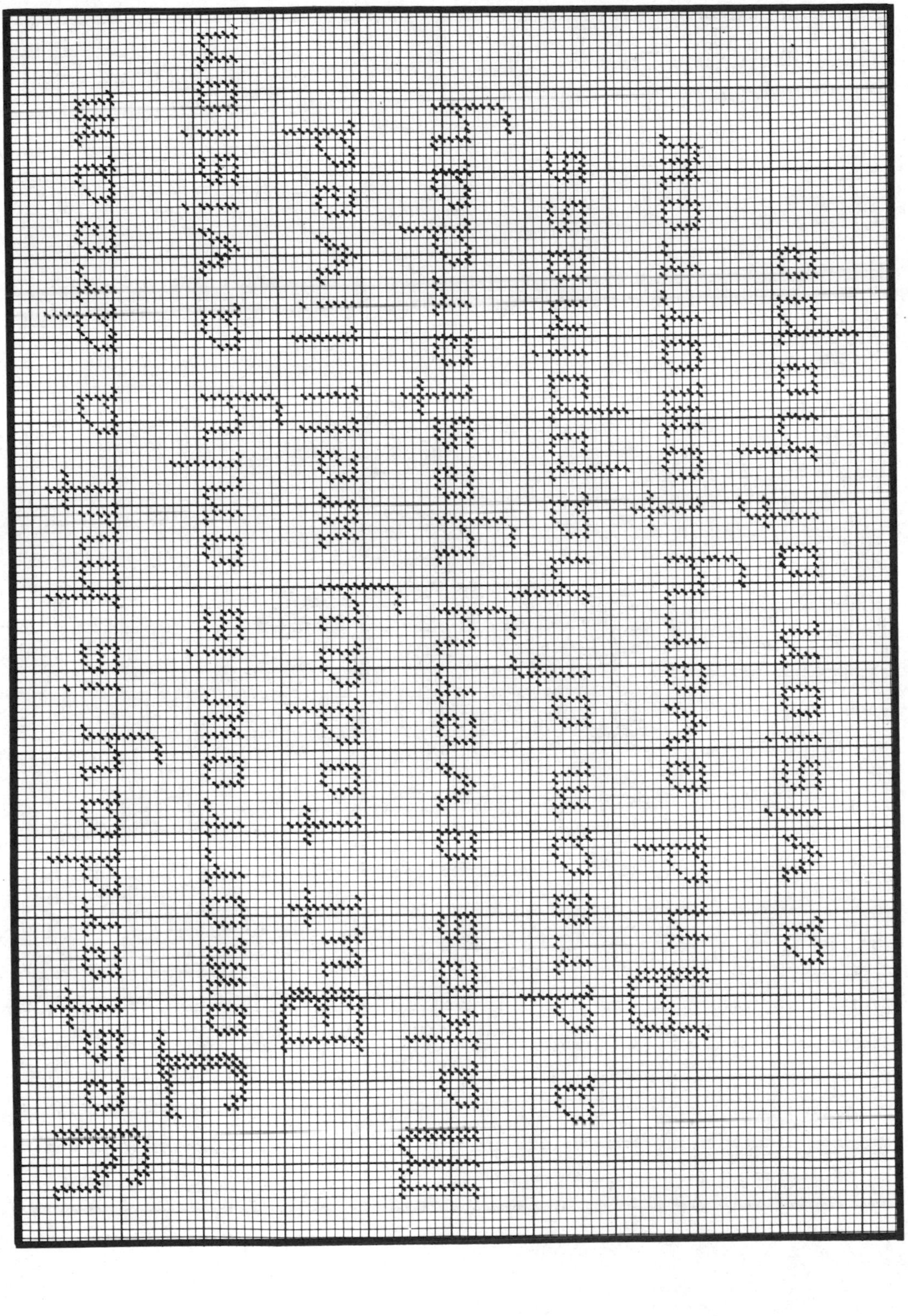
Yesterday is but a dream
Tomorrow is only a vision
But today well lived
makes every yesterday
a dream of happiness
And every tomorrow
a vision of hope

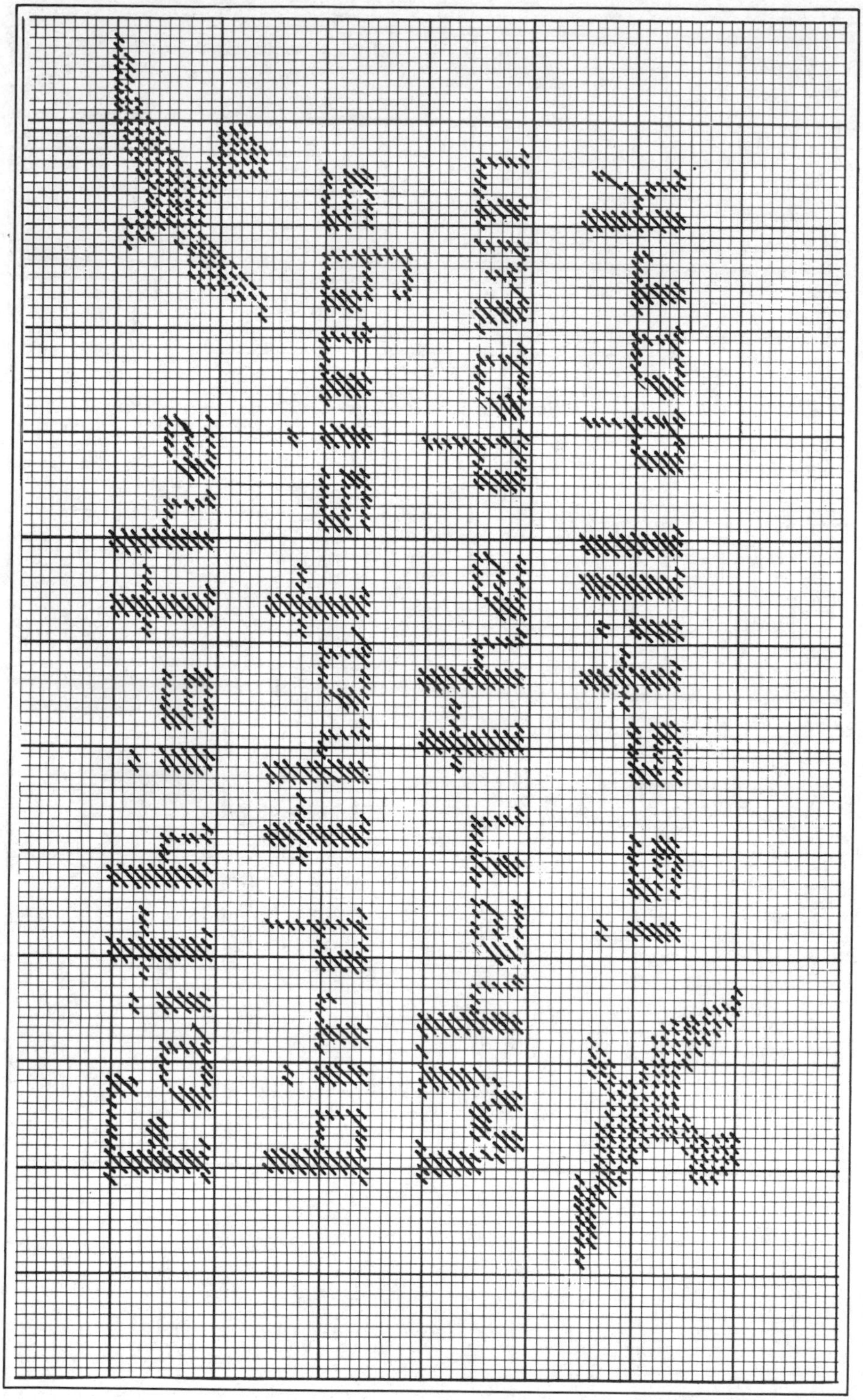

For the Handicapped

Over the years, I have received many letters from people with various handicaps who have found great solace and joy in needlecraft. What a shame that I did not save them all. Instead, when the decision was made to include a chapter with suggestions for the handicapped in this book, I asked my readers to send me their suggestions. From the many letters sent, and from a few old ones still on file, this chapter was formed. Whether or not you have had to overcome a physical handicap, I think you will find many of these heartwarming. Some of the letters have been edited to avoid duplication.

Perhaps your readers would like to hear about some of the devices I have used since having a stroke about four years ago.

After spending one full day trying to thread yarn into a needle, my husband cut a few hundred used envelopes into inch-long strips along the folded edges, making them just wide enough to go through the eye of a tapestry needle. By laying the yarn inside the folded strip, I was able to thread the needle easily.

An old picture frame that fits across the arms of my chair served as a "holder" for my canvas. My husband would thumb-tack the canvas to the frame, and then I was ready to proceed. Since then, I have found needlepoint frames in craft catalogs.

I used to paint but now can't hold a brush too well, so I do my "painting" with yarn, making my own designs.

To knit again, I tried using size 50 needles and simple pattern stitches such as "knit 4, purl 4" for four rows and then reversing for the next four rows. After this became comfortable, I changed to size 30 needles and, after several months of gradually moving down to smaller needles, I can now use even size 2!

Part of the time I had to use my left hand to tighten the grip of my right hand on the needle.

I am able to walk now, but for quite a while I was in a wheelchair with my right side completely paralyzed. I quickly tired of reading so have tried very hard with crafts.

—Mrs. C. Coppock, Garden City, South Carolina

Several years ago, I smashed my left arm in a fall on the ice. Surgery was required, followed by eight weeks in a cast, and then physical therapy for most of the rest of the year. I eventually regained most of the use of my arm.

During the period of my recovery, when I was taking physical therapy and doing exercises every day, I was exposed to macrame for the first time. An acquaintance was teaching a class, and I had nothing to lose by trying it out.

I started a belt that I never finished because the class was discontinued, but the lessons did succeed in introducing me to macrame and providing therapy.

The instructor didn't use a macrame board but instead told me to attach the piece of work to a door knob. I remember sitting there forcing my fingers to make the knots and pulling on the strands with what little strength I had. I am sure that this was a beneficial activity because anything that helped increase the function of my arm and hand was helpful.

I have seen others squeezing balls for therapy, but I think that an activity that has visible results gives much more satisfaction and is equally therapeutic, if not more so. For example, medical personnel advised me to sit on the edge of my bed and exercise my fingers. I said, "Ridiculous!" Instead, I forced my fingers and arms to move on a real piano keyboard.

I would think that stroke and arthritis patients could benefit from these practical, therapeutic activities as well. This is what occupational therapy is all about. The hospital where I was a patient didn't have an occupational therapy department at that time, so I was forced to depend on my own creativity for therapy.—Marilyn Baker, Warwick, Rhode Island

I am the home skills specialist at Work Adjustment Services in Neenah, Wisconsin, where we enroll mentally and physically handicapped adults. In part of this program, I teach handicraft

classes that include needlepoint, rug hooking, embroidery, and crewel.

I could not find an instruction manual of needlework for the retarded, so I have developed large sample cards with arrows and/or numbers to show the directions for various needlepoint stitches.

For needlepoint, I find the large-mesh plastic canvas and large-eye tapestry needle the best. The canvas won't stretch, and it is much easier to remove mistakes without damaging the canvas. Patterns are a problem—the less detail in the pattern the better it is for low functioning individuals. Even with higher functioning individuals, however, written directions do not work as well as enlarged sample cards in teaching needlepoint.

In rug hooking, the clients do purchase commercially printed rug kits. For latchhook, I have found the curved bottom latchhook easier to use than the straight edge type—the yarn can easily be placed under the hook without getting the previous yarn tangled.

One thing I watch for in purchasing the kits is that the color key matches the actual color of the yarn. Otherwise, I find it difficult to explain why dark blue yarn is used for the blue markings and light blue yarn for green markings.
—Lee A. Van Hulle, Work Adjustment Services, Inc., Neenah, Wisconsin

Since developing arthritis in my right hand, I have mastered the art of crocheting by using a different "hold" on my crochet hooks. The usual grip of a hook, taught in most needlecraft manuals, is like that of holding a pencil in a writing posture. I have found it less strenuous on my wrist and fingers to assume a grip on the hook similar to that of holding a knife to cut meat on a plate. It works very well with larger hooks and heavy yarns, but, with practice, one can eventually work even with the fine crochet cottons.—Lillian Perkins, Leicester, New York

Many people wrote suggesting that masking (or similar) tape could be wrapped round and round the center of the crochet hook to build it up in order to make it easier for crippled hands to hold. There is, however, one hook on the market that is curved, has a large handle, and is much easier to hold than the ordinary hook. Ask your craft shop about the availability of "handi hooks."

*

As a polio victim of long standing (50 years), I know that needlework is of great value in making one happy, and it is good and pleasant exercise for the muscles still in use.

The interest in a craft, however, must come first, then the desire to do comes when you see a pretty pattern or design you want to make.

I like crocheting, myself, and now have quite good use of my right arm, which was once completely paralyzed. I think crocheting helped bring movement back to my arm. When I was first able to move the arm at all, I could only stretch crepe paper and play with a light celluloid doll. As soon as I could move my hand, my mother taught me to crochet and perhaps that is why crocheting is still my favorite needlework activity. Later, I learned to knit, tat, make rugs, and do other arts and crafts.

I think the best needlework for the handicapped is simply whatever they like to do best. I have seen a girl with one arm do beautiful reweaving, people with crippled hands do latch hook rugs and needlepoint, and people with severe arthritis in their hands do beautiful sewing and make dolls.

Personally, I love to do mending and alterations as it gives me joy to fix something and make it useful again. I love to experiment or "play" with colors. This for me is better than a pain pill when the weather is damp and I am achy. My mother used to say, "Get interested in something, and you won't mind the pain so much." It worked.

Years later, I learned that concentrating on something you enjoy—whether it be needlework, music, books, cooking, or whatever—does block the pain by raising the pain threshold. You might still have pain, but you are not as aware of it because you are thinking of something else and concentrating on that.

Lap frames or floor frames are good for people who have only one good hand. A table or tea cart the right height for a work surface is very useful. I prefer a tea cart because I can push it to a window with the right light; also the foot rests of my wheelchair will fit in over the lower shelf of the cart allowing me to get close to the work area. It is like an arts and crafts center on wheels.

I have a small cart purchased a year or two ago for less than $25. It is wonderful and can be used for a portable typewriter or sewing machine, as a needlepoint carrier, for carting plants to a sunny window, and for all sorts of work around the kitchen or dining area.

They are so useful that I just wish I had two or three of them. I even push mine out on the balcony on a sunny day.

I have seen beautiful doll clothes and miniatures made by the handicapped. I think smaller projects are easier where strength and energy are a problem. But the handicapped are even tackling mountains now.

Finally, I might mention a magazine for the handicapped, *Accent on Living.* Their address is: P.O. Box 700, Bloomington, Illinois, 61701. For years, I have found the magazine to be a good source of aids and information for the handicapped.

—Virginia Brodner, Redondo Beach, California

The following letter was received and reproduced in one of my columns in August of 1979:

Several members of The Guild for the Blind in Chicago have noticed your column in our newspaper. Can you please help us alert your readers to the availability of craft and hobby books for their blind friends and relatives?

The "Self-Help Series" was written and designed by the blind for the blind and is a confidence-building program. These materials are produced at a much higher price than they are sold for.

We would like this series mentioned as a resource for the blind or visually impaired, of which the elderly are the fastest growing segment.

Your mention of this would make it possible to reach many who would otherwise not know about these materials. Thank you for your consideration.—Kevin Lynch, The Guild for the Blind, 180 N. Michigan Avenue, Suite 1720, Chicago, Illinois 60601

Among the manuals available are ones on macrame, sewing, and latch hooking, all available in braille, large print, or cassettes. There are others to help the blind care for indoor plants, bake breads, or cook a variety of recipes.

Although the guild is headquartered in Chicago, it is a national organization and will supply information on the materials available to anyone, anywhere. Just write to the guild at the address given in the previous letter for further information.

For Chicago-area residents, the guild offers a course in braille transcribing to sighted volunteers. If you live elsewhere and would like to become a braille transcriber, check with your local association for the blind. This type of instruction is offered in many areas.

In the past, some local associations for the blind have requested my permission to reproduce one or more of my instruction leaflets in braille. I am always happy to give the permission and will also send complimentary copies of any leaflet if I receive the request on the letterhead of such an organization.

I think that many of us who are blessed with sight do not realize that beautiful handwork can be done by those who can no longer see. When we think of the great pleasure gained through creative crafts, just imagine how much more this must mean to those living in a sightless world.

As a nurse disabled with a back injury for the last few years, I was so glad to see you take an interest in problems for the handicapped.

Since my injury, I have become an avid knitter—to keep myself busy and to create new challenges. What I needed was a craft that I could perform while lying on my back.

Knitting had been a hobby of mine years ago when our children were small, so I decided to try it again. Because of a limited tolerance for sitting, I encountered several problems and found some solutions that fit my needs.

Straight knitting needles are unsuitable in over a 10-inch length as the needles catch in the arms of a chair or wheelchair. The longer needles also force you to elevate your arms, which causes fatigue when in a prone position.

I learned to use circular needles for all of my knitting and switched to what you call Continental knitting, holding the yarn in the left hand. This prevents the fatigue encountered when "throwing" the yarn with the right hand. Even tension was a problem, but with practice my work became more even and smooth. Having finished my first Fair Isle cardigan, I can honestly say that this Continental knitting style really paid off.

A large, sturdy knitting bag is a must to keep yarn, needles, markers, tape measures, etc., together. For a bedridden or wheelchair-bound patient, having things close at hand and at a reachable height is very important.

Handling patterns and pattern books also presented problems. Hardcover books are fine for reading, but awkward to use for following a pattern. I solved this problem by having the pages of the pattern reproduced on a copy machine. I then put the pages in a three-hole plastic page holder that allows the directions to show on both sides. A paper clip and a small piece of paper attached to the plastic holder is handy for marking down the rows as you work or to make notes.

Obtaining patterns is also difficult when you are unable to go to a store yourself. My chief sources have been from friends who knit or from newspaper columns such as yours.

I prefer to use instructions for garments started at the neck and knitted to the bottom for better individual fit. I like the challenge of using odds and ends of leftover yarn to make small items. Large projects such as afghans are difficult to handle because of the weight. Patterns that can be worked individually and then joined are much easier to handle.

—Carolee Wood, Clarence, New York

✳

Having been a paraplegic for 32 years, I have some ideas that might be helpful to others. I do have the full use of my arms and hands, so some of the tips will be for everyone.

For machine sewing, my husband took my sewing machine head and installed it in a counter at the exact height for my wheelchair. The machine folds down into the counter just as in a console. A section that matches the rest of the counter slips over the downed machine to make a desk.

To sew, I place the foot pedal on the counter and press it with my right elbow, thus freeing my hands to guide the fabric.

Using this method, I have made everything from a Merry Widow to go under my daughter's formal to tailored couch covers and even Ultrasuede garments. I tried making a tent once, but the machine couldn't handle it!

I store all my yarns in 3-pound coffee cans. Each is labeled and stored on easy-to-reach shelves, and the yarn is kept clean and mothproof.

For large quantities of yarn, I use 25-pound detergent boxes with lids. I cover these with contact paper.

For my needlepoint and crewel yarns, I have a commercially made purse and lingerie holder that hangs from a closet rod. The hanger swivels, so it is easy to unzip the see-through pockets. This bag could also be used for sewing supplies or almost any needlecraft supply need.

An upcoming project for me is spinning. I have a hand-held spindle and can hardly wait to collect enough Great Pyrenees wool from our dog to complete a garment!

—Sylvia Jones, Seattle, Washington

✳

I do a lot of knitting and have difficulty seeing numbers on those little row counters one puts on a knitting needle. I use one of those clickety-clack gadgets designed for use in markets when shopping.

I use the first two numbers for stitches going across and the last two numbers for rows. It works fine, and I have no difficulty seeing those numbers because they are nice and big. I keep my "handy counter" right on the table where I do my knitting.

Also, for people who have only the use of one arm, a small vise clamped to an adjustable ironing board placed in front of a person will hold embroidery hoops for crewel or frame for needlepoint and is much cheaper than buying a standing frame.

If threading a needle is difficult, dip the end of the thread in Elmer's glue. It hardens in a second and stiffens the thread so it will go through the eye easily.

—Evelyn Smith, Seekonk, Massachusetts

I have always done a lot of knitting and crocheting, but a year ago my hands became very swollen and painful and have remained that way.

I bought a small wrist pincushion and put it in the palm of my hand. That keeps my hand from closing, keeps the needles in position, and eliminates any extra pain. I hope this invention of mine helps someone else.

—Leah Willard, Doylestown, Pennsylvania

My mother is now blind but did crochet before she lost her sight. She has just recently started to crochet again, however, using a simple afghan pattern that requires no sewing together and no shaping. She uses an ordinary safety pin to keep her place. She puts it into the last loop when removing her hook. The head of the pin is pointed in the direction she is working, so that she will know which direction to work in when she picks her work up again.—Theresa Stewart, Gambrills, Maryland

My mother had a stroke when she was 62 and then lived with a paralyzed right arm for 18 years. She learned to write with her left hand but got very bored with not being able to do much. So I got her started doing cross-stitch on gingham, which was popular in the sixties. She made a number of aprons and square-dance skirts.

From there we went on to embroidering tea towels, pillowcases, samplers, bedspreads, and tablecloths. In the 18 years, she completed around 250 items. The last year of her life, we entered some of her things in the county fair, and she won many red and blue ribbons for her work.

At first she could not master threading the needles, so she kept a supply that Dad would thread before he left the house. Before she could master using a hoop, she used a heavy piece of embossed plastic, which she put under her work to stitch against. She used her thread until it was very short, and she didn't use knots. Her work was very neat and beautiful. Family members and friends have many treasures today.

She later learned to thread needles and use a hoop. A crochet hook was used to get out the tangles or sometimes to fasten a thread. Left-handed scissors were a must—as was her determination. In the five years that she lived after Dad died suddenly of a heart attack, she spent many hours embroidering.

—Betty Kemper, Omaha, Nebraska

I would like to tell you about my husband's handiwork. Because of emphysema, he couldn't do anything strenuous, so he took up latch-hooking. Starting with small kits, he gradually worked up to making rugs.

After suffering a broken arm last year, he could no longer work on his rugs, so he bought a small kit to do in "long stitch." This worked so well he decided to try other needlepoint.

He's been teaching and encouraging other disabled men to do these projects too, and they are also doing well.

I, being an avid needleworker, feel that more of our handicapped folks, or even just retirees, need to be encouraged to work on projects for their own enjoyment and to while away the many lonely hours.—Bertha Bryer, Mapleville, Rhode Island

Finally, I asked Lana Ford, associate professor of the occupational therapy department at Western Michigan University, to review these helpful letters from my readers. She was kind enough to offer her own expert advice and tips:

In reading the letters from your readers, I must say there are a great many creative folks around—enough so that I might soon be out of a job as an occupational therapist. There are many good ideas and I agree that "what works" is "what works best." There aren't any right or wrong ways of adjusting to a disability. I won't repeat any of the suggestions already made but would like to offer a few more ideas.

Positioning is very important to avoid fatigue. If sitting for a long time, try elevating the feet, but not too much. Use foot rests or prop feet on a box—sitting straight-legged can cause stiffness in the knees. Also try putting a pillow under the knees or between them. Keeping the legs apart at the hips with the knees slightly bent is most relaxing.

Work in good light to avoid eye strain, especially with close work. Non-glare or "soft-light" bulbs are better to reduce glare from printed patterns. When possible, use the natural lighting by positioning the work area close to a window.

If pattern books are copyrighted, many authors give permission when filing for copyright to have books printed in large print, braille, or phono records. For information give the title of the book and date of publication to the Library of Congress, Copyright Division, Washington, D.C. 20559. Most are available free or for a low cost. Information is also available from local libraries and the local Chapter for the Blind.

In completing needlepoint, quilting, or embroidery many people have learned to do the stitching with the same hand that they write with. But if that hand is somewhat impaired due to a stroke or arthritis, it may be difficult to completely switch and learn new skills with the other hand. If the involved hand is usable but fatigues quickly, try a two-handed method of stitching. One hand works on the top of the fabric to push the needle back up through the fabric. This method allows for many repetitions in grasp and release as the hands work alternately. Worked in this manner, the activity is really "therapeutic" and much more fun than doing exercises.

Latch-hook commercial kits often have yarn too short to grasp tightly. A pre-printed pattern may be purchased separately or a self-made pattern can be created. To create your own pattern trace a picture from a magazine with tracing paper. Use indelible carbon to transfer the design to the canvas. Color code the canvas with indelible pens or acrylic paint. (Don't use crayons or felt pens as the colors come off on the yarn.) Then measure the yarn to the desired length (once it has been latched it can always be trimmed if it is too long). Wrap the yarn around two nails pounded in a board 4 inches apart. Cut at each end. The 4-inch strands of yarn are much easier to handle. Completion of a project in this manner also requires use of scissors, pencils, and some careful pre-planning.

Build up the handles of tools (such as punch rug tools, knitting needles, or crochet hooks) for easier grasp. Wrap a washrag or a rag to desired thickness and tape it securely with masking tape. An old Ace bandage works well too.

Position all needed supplies on a non-slip surface. Dycem matting comes in pads 10 inches by 14, 10, or 8 inches and is great for placing on a T.V. tray. This non-slip matting is available from Fred Sammons, Inc., Box 32, Brookfield, Illinois 60513. Silverware trays also make inexpensive compartmental storage for lengths of yarn, scissors, needles, buttons, and so forth.

In addition to positioning materials, make sure the work is secured. If no one is available to stretch materials or canvas, try using large clips from old clipboards or clips from a local office supply store. Velcro is a material that comes in 1-inch strips with a loop and a hook self-sticking pile. Small pieces can be sewn to the fabric to be stretched, with the companion strip glued to the frame. Velcro is available from Fred Sammons and can also be found in most local stores that carry sewing supplies.

If strength is a problem, think about the resistance of the material. Burlap has a more open weave for embroidery and punch rug. Wools used in needlepoint are often harder to work with than synthetic yarns or polyester yarns. Embroidery floss that is smooth may be substituted for any form of yarn in completing needlepoint. It will also give the finished project a softer look, yet will be as durable.

Some initial planning should be done before attempting any craft activity. It is very discouraging to select a craft activity and be forced to abandon it before it is completed due to fatigue or frustration. But the real problem might not be the amount of disability—perhaps the wrong activity was selected. For example, knitting, latch-hook rugs, and macrame are two-handed activities. That means both hands do the same thing or the hands work together performing different functions. Conversely, needlepoint, crochet, and punch rug are really one-handed activities—the other hand acts mostly to hold or stabilize the work. When one hand primarily holds, this function can be substituted artificially by securing the work in a frame. Be good observers and ask salespersons in stores *how* different crafts are done before making the initial selection. Explore other kinds of craft activities such as dried flower arrangements or shell craft. These latter two activities involve materials that are very light weight. Both can be used to decorate small boxes or can be placed in picture frames. This kind of activity may also involve some exploration of the general area to gather materials. Walking in a field or on the beach can be as therapeutic as the activity of creating a project from found materials.

Regardless of the nature of the needlework or craft activity two general principles should be observed. First, work from simple to complex. In needlepoint, begin with the plastic canvas before quick point. Begin with patterns that are geometric to allow mastery of stitching before attempting to do an intricate floral design. Start latch hook with a pillow before attempting a large rug or a wall hanging. Knit a lap cover before an afghan or a sweater. This ensures mastery of basic skills and helps build self-confidence. Smaller projects also have fewer component skills. For example, in knitting a sweater, one also must size the finished pieces and sew them together.

The second principle is similar to the first—work from gross to fine or big to little. Concentrate on activities that will allow motions in the shoulder, elbow, and wrist before selecting activities that require fine movements of the fingers. This is a simple principle that applies to the development of all skills, either in learning skills for the first time or in regaining skills that have been lost. Just watch a small infant and notice that long before he is able to stack blocks and pick up small objects, there is a lot of random arm waving. This suggests that some of the first projects should be mounted vertically, which requires working in a position with some forward movement at the shoulders. This implies that some work is done with the elbow outstretched in reaching. Macrame is an excellent activity that provides motion of the shoulder, elbow, wrist, and hands when the ropes being worked on are suspended from a hook in a door frame.

All too often, many people begin working on projects immediately following the onset of a disability and in fact do regain much of the use of their hand—as long as that hand is positioned in the lap. But the hand may be nonusable when attempting to perform other household activities like cooking, dressing, or doing the laundry. It must be remembered the hand is basically a prehension tool attached to the arm. Unless that arm can move, the tool is useless. And it is precisely that tool that can help in regaining a useful and productive life.

—Lana Ford, associate professor, occupational therapy
department, Western Michigan University

Bibliography

Ambuter, Carolyn. *Complete Book of Needlepoint.* New York: Thomas Y. Crowell, 1972.

Bucher, Jo. *Creative Needlepoint.* Des Moines: Creative Home Library, 1973.

Burchette, Dorothy. *Needlework Blocking and Finishing.* New York: Scribner's, 1981.

Burns, Hildy Paige, and Kathleen Thorne-Thomsen. *American Cross Stitch.* New York: Van Nostrand Reinhold, 1974.

Chatterton, Pauline. *Gobelin Stitch Embroidery.* New York: Scribner's, 1980.

Christensen, Jo A. *The Needlepoint Book.* Englewood Cliffs, N.J.: Prentice-Hall, 1976.

———. *Needlepoint, The Third Dimension.* Englewood Cliffs, N.J.: Prentice-Hall, 1979.

Donnelly, Barbara H. *The Crewel Needlepoint World.* Sweden: Ljungforetagen, 1973.

Fischer, P., and Lasker, A. *Bargello Magic.* New York: Holt, Rinehard & Winston, 1972.

Gostelow, Mary. *A World of Embroidery.* New York: Scribner's, 1975.

———. *Blackwork.* New York: Van Nostrand Reinhold, 1977.

Guild, Vera P. *Good Housekeeping Needlecraft.* New York: Hearst Books, 1971.

Hall, N., and Riley, J. *Bargello Borders.* Franklin, Mich.: Needlemania, 1974.

Hanley, Hope. *Needlepoint.* New York: Scribner's, 1975.

———. *Needlepoint Rugs.* New York: Scribner's, 1971.

Kaestner, Dorothy. *Bargello Antics.* New York: Scribner's, 1979.

Katzenburg, Gloria. *Needlepoint and Pattern.* New York: Macmillan, 1974.

Lane, Maggie. *Rugs and Wall Hangings.* New York: Scribner's, 1981.

Lantz, Shirlee. *A Pageant of Pattern for Needlepoint.* New York: Grosset & Dunlap, 1973.

Neilsen, Edith, *Scandinavian Embroidery, Past and Present.* New York: Scribner's, 1978.

Orr, Jan. *Now Needlepoint.* New York: Van Nostrand Reinhold, 1975.

Perrone, Lizbeth. *The New World of Needlepoint.* New York: Random House, 1972.

Projansky, Ella. *Sculptured Needlepoint Stitchery.* New York: Scribner's, 1981.

Rhodes, Mary. *Dictionary of Canvas Work Stitches.* New York: Scribner's, 1980.

Ryan, Mildred Groves. *The Complete Encyclopedia of Stitchery.* Garden City, N.Y.: Doubleday, 1979.

Scheuer, Nikki. *Designs for Bargello.* Garden City, N.Y.: Doubleday, 1973.

———. *Designs for Holbein Embroidery.* Garden City, N.Y.: Doubleday, 1976.

Sorensen, Grethe. *Needlepoint Designs from Oriental Rugs.* New York: Scribner's, 1981.

BIBLIOGRAPHY

Stevens, Gigs. *Free Form Bargello*. New York: Scribner's, 1977.
Weal, Michele. *Texture and Color in Needlepoint*. New York: Harper & Row, 1975.
Williams, Elsa. *Bargello, Florentine Canvas Work*. New York: Van Nostrand Reinhold, 1967.
Wilson, Erica. *Needleplay*. New York: Scribner's, 1975.
Winter, Adalee. *Needlepoint Kingdom*. Birmingham, Ala.: Oxmoor House, 1975.

Index

References to charts or diagrams are in **bold**.